Haven't You Heard?
There's a WAR
Going On!

Unlocking the Code to Revelation

Haven't You Heard?
There's a WAR
Going On!

Unlocking the Code to Revelation

ELDRED ECHOLS

(Doug Allen's teacher at)
MCC.

— *A* —
FAITH FOCUS
Book

Sweet Publishing
Fort Worth, Texas

Haven't You Heard? There's a WAR Going On!
Unlocking the Code to Revelation

Library of Congress Catalog Number 92-61653

ISBN: 0-8344-0225-4

Printed in the U. S. A.
10   9   8   7   6   5   4   3   2

Contents

Babylon is Falling   Claude Witty

Essential Keys to Revelation

No book has so captured the imaginations of men or caused as much speculation as the Revelation of Jesus Christ, recorded by the apostle John. Its dazzling images and symbolic language allow for a wide range of unique interpretations and strange doctrines. (See Methods for Interpreting Revelation, Appendix 1, in the back of this book for further explanation.)

Because of its "end times" (eschatological) language, Revelation is often cited as proof text for wild speculation on the end of the world and God's kingdom. This approach has created endless debate about the identity of the beast, about who will fight the battle of Armageddon, and about what the end of the world will be like, to name a few. While many are caught up in the interpreting of world events, the vast majority of Christians have neglected the study of Revelation. They feel that they will never be able to understand its true meaning—which has probably been lost and, therefore, is now irrelevant.

Revelation actually was written in a secret code that was unknown even to many Christians of that day. A brief review of history in the apostle John's day reveals a need for the coded message and a system for its proper interpretation.

Irenaeus was a prominent second-century Christian scholar who had been trained by Polycarp, a personal disciple of John. Irenaeus tells us that the tyrant Domitian imprisoned John on the Isle of Patmos in A.D. 95 for his Christian activities. The authorities were confident that by removing John from the scene, the Christians would falter and soon disclaim their allegiance to Christ and his emerging church. At the end of the first century Christians were under more widespread persecution than ever before, and they could not understand what had gone wrong. Had Satan won the battle? Was the church going to be overcome by evil? If not, when would the tide turn and God take charge? It was in response to this crisis of faith that Revelation was written.

The Christians did need John's message of encouragement and motivation, but how could he possibly get it to them? There was a way—a coded message that could be interpreted by most Jewish followers of Christ, yet appear totally meaningless to their Roman persecutors. John was surely laying all these conditions and concerns before the Father in prayer when the Holy Spirit came to him with the Revelation.

Revelation's reliance upon the Hebrew apocalyptic symbols and the Hebrew mystic numbers system allowed Jewish Christians, who were all over the known world as a result of the great dispersion mentioned in Acts 8, to interpret the message for their Gentile brothers and sisters.

These specific symbols and numbers and their meanings had been handed down from generation to generation as the Jewish priests and fathers interpreted the mystical Old Testament writings of Isaiah, Ezekiel, and Daniel.

Most of the Jewish nation never had access to the actual written scrolls, and so it was imperative that they commit to memory these scriptures and essential keys to understanding the old prophecies.

Having complete access to ancient history and, of course, the Old and New Testaments, today's Christians can once again unlock the code to John's secret message.

These specific keys will help open this book for you:

Key # 1: Old Testament prophecies and visions and the teachings of Jesus.

About one hundred quotations and allusions from the Old Testament's prophetic and apocalyptic books are used in Revelation. Therefore, it's impossible to understand much of the book's content without considerable reference to the prophetic literature of the Old Testament. Ezekiel, Daniel, and Isaiah are referred to heavily, with some references made to Zechariah. For example, John uses Jesus' teachings from these Old Testament books when he refers to Matthew 24:29, 30 (" '. . . the sun will be darkened, and the moon will not give its light; the stars will fall from the sky, and the heavenly bodies will be shaken. . . .' ") in Revelation 6:12, 13 (". . . The sun turned black like sackcloth made of goat hair, the whole moon turned blood red, and the stars in the sky fell to earth . . .").

Key # 2: Apocalyptic symbols.

Most of these symbols are common to Hebrew apocalyptic literature. The Old Testament prophets used them. They were also popular in Hebrew literature outside the Bible, written during the time between the writing of Malachi and the writing of the Gospels. Following are some common symbols and their meanings. For additional apocalyptic terms, see the Glossary in the back of this book as well as the Chapter Keys at the beginning of each chapter.

Armageddon (literally, **"Mount Megiddo"**) is the code word for an ultimate struggle between good and evil.

beast symbolizes a power or institution—political or religious—which is hostile to God and his children (see also Daniel 7:3–8:4).

dragon represents Satan (Genesis 3).

earth is the representation of the world system (or sometimes Judaism when contrasted with *sea,* but most often as above).

eyes are the symbol for knowledge (1 Kings 23:43; Zechariah 4:10).

horns most often represent powers or kings (2 Samuel 22:3; Jeremiah 48:25; Lamentations 2:3, 17; Daniel 8:3-21).

lamb is the symbol for Christ—the sacrificial offering for sin (Isaiah 53:7; John 1:29).

lamps stand for truth (Psalm 119:105; Proverbs 6:23).

mountains represent kingdoms (2 Chronicles 20:10; Daniel 2:35; 9:16; Micah 4:1). Ancient "kingdoms" of the Middle East were often little more than fortified cities built upon the highest point of land in the area. So, the term "mountain" symbolizes a community of strength—a kingdom.

sea symbolizes the pagan world (Daniel 7:3).

serpent	represents Satan (Genesis 3).
throne	represents authority (Proverbs 20:28; Isaiah 14:13; Jeremiah 3:17).

Key # 3: Hebrew mystic numbers.

As in most ancient (and some modern) civilizations, numbers and numerology were considered powerful and important mysteries—quite apart from their simple arithmetical values. The frequent numerical symbols in Revelation derive their importance from this practice.

three	From ancient times, the number three has represented deity. Plato (the greatest of all Greek philosophers) and Philo (an influential Jewish philosopher of the first century A.D.) both comment upon this remarkable fact. There were triads of deities in most ancient religions (Egyptian, Babylonian, and Vedic Hinduism are examples). Often there were multiple minor gods, but only three principal ones. Some philosophers believed the number three suggested that God was the beginning, middle, and end of everything, or that three was an expression of God's eternity—past, present, and future. But, for whatever reason, three is the God-number, the symbol of the Godhead.
four	Four is the number of the earth or the material universe. In the 3,000 years before Christ, the Babylonian rulers had the title, Ruler of the Four Quarters of

the Earth. Time was determined by the four phases of the moon. The year was divided into four seasons. The Bible speaks of the "four winds," and all peoples use the four cardinal points of the compass: north, south, east, and west. Ancient peoples divided the animal creation into four classes, and their zodiac had four signs. There were four rivers bordering Eden, and there were four angels of destruction. And on it goes. Four, then, is the earth number—the number of the physical universe and the number of humanity in its earthly setting.

seven The number seven, as used in Revelation, symbolizes salvation or the Savior. There are seven spirits, seven lampstands, seven churches, seven stars, seven angels, seven trumpets, and so on. It appears most likely that this use of seven is derived from four added to three—man (four) joined to the Godhead (three)—thus equal to man saved. Jesus himself is both God and man (a sum of seven again), and his mission of rejoining man to God is a sum of seven. An exception to this "seven-principle" is the apostate church, an imposter promising a salvation it cannot deliver. In Revelation it masquerades under the number seven.

ten The number ten represents abstract completeness (a perfection of quality, rather than numerical completeness).

Ten expresses the ultimate degree of anything, whether extremely good and holy or extremely bad and wicked. The dimensions of the tabernacle were based upon ten. Ten righteous men would have saved Sodom. Jacob complained that his wages were changed ten times. There were ten plagues, and God gave Israel the Ten Commandments. The high priest prayed ten times on the Day of Atonement; ten was the proper number of persons for a Passover meal; ten men were required as the quorum to form a new synagogue. Ten were needed to mourn at a funeral or to celebrate in a wedding party. Jesus used the number ten frequently: ten servants, ten talents, ten coins, ten cities, ten virgins, ten times ten (one hundred) sheep in the Good Shepherd's flock, and so forth. Ten was the number symbolic of the full degree of anything.

twelve Twelve was the number of concrete completeness—everyone or everything present and accounted for. The Jewish importance of this symbol probably originated in the twelve sons of Jacob who became the fathers of the twelve tribes of Israel—the whole of the nation. Moses set up twelve pillars. There were twelve jewels in the breastplate of the high priest, twelve cakes of shewbread in the ark of the covenant, twelve spies, twelve memorial stones, twelve officers of Solomon, twelve stones in Elijah's altar, twelve apostles, and twelve gates of paradise. Twelve is the symbol for the presence of all God's chosen ones.

one thousand

Since ten is the number of abstract completeness, the ultimate degree of perfection would be achieved by raising it to the third power—especially so, since three, as stated above, is the representation of God. Ten times ten times ten is one thousand, completeness infused with divinity—absolute perfection. One thousand was the number of the messianic kingdom anticipated by the Jews before the coming of Christ because it was the place where God would dwell with all his people. The rabbis taught that "the days of the Messiah are a thousand years." The Talmud states that "the righteous shall fly above the waters [the pagan world] a thousand years." Pagan writers also used this number to refer to existence after death. Plato, in the *Republic* and Virgil in the *Aeneid* make use of such symbolism. The cube of the measurement of the holy of holies (where God dwelled with his people) was one thousand. By extending this concept, the realm or state where God dwells with his people can be expressed as "a thousand years."

As a summary of these mystic symbols and numbers, consider Revelation 5:6. Jesus is there portrayed as a **lamb** with **seven horns** and **seven eyes**—a way of saying that Jesus shed his blood sacrificially for us, and that he has both the power and the knowledge to provide salvation. His **eyes** are said to be the **seven** spirits of God which are sent out to all the earth. That is, Jesus effected our salvation by the saving truth of the Gospel, sent out by the power of the Holy Spirit into all the world.

One final point should prove beneficial. Revelation is not written in a chronological order. The messages are repeated, sometimes more than once, and become cyclical in nature. Always though, the message is the same. There is a fierce war raging between the armies of Christ and Satan for the soul of every human being. For those who remain in Christ's army the final outcome has already been determined. Victory is in Jesus!

Chapter Keys

crown   *symbolizes great honor or power.*

dragon   *represents Satan.*

horns   *most often represent powers or kings.*

serpent   *represents Satan.*

star   *symbolizes heralds or messengers. They were also considered lesser lights (important, but inferior to the great lights of sun and moon).*

time, times and half a time
indicates a system which cannot offer salvation.

7   *symbolizes salvation or the Savior. This use of seven is derived from four added to three—man (four) joined to God (three); man saved. Jesus himself is both God and man (a sum of seven again), and his mission of rejoining man to God is a sum of seven.*

Chapter 1

The Ultimate War

Armageddon

∽

Revelation 16; 19; 20

Key Message:

The human spirit is the real arena for this war.

High Noon. Gunfight at the O.K. Corral. Custer's Last Stand. The Alamo. The Bridge at Concord. The Shot Heard 'Round the World. And finally, the ultimate—The Battle of Armageddon. Isn't there something thrilling about the notion of a confrontation between two mighty foes—a stand-off from which there will be no retreat, a fight to the finish, which only one side can possibly survive? John gives us such an image in his revelation of hope. In fact, the word he uses has become a modern-day symbol for a huge, decisive battle between the forces of light and darkness—*Armageddon*.

Few concepts have so excited the imaginations, hopes, and fears of millions of people as the idea of a

12

Haven't You Heard? There's a WAR Going On! _____

great battle of cosmic size known as Armageddon. Even the average man on the street, who is only slightly religious, knows about the battle of Armageddon. He may have no idea of where the concept comes from and little notion of what it means. He is only vaguely aware that it's about some spectacular upheaval featuring the angels themselves, and it could begin any time.

The truth is, the battle of Armageddon has already begun. Haven't you heard? There's a *war* going on! And you're in the middle of it.

The Real Battle of Armageddon

Not against flesh and blood. People who are anxiously expecting a worldwide war that will herald the end of the world are as misdirected as the Pharisees of the first century were. The Israelites had waited in confident hope for fifteen centuries. Yet, they were so blinded by their own false goals that they missed the Messiah when he did come. What a tragedy to wait fifteen centuries for their moment of glory on the stage of history—and then to miss their cue!

In the same way, some people are carefully evaluating every "war and rumor of war" as a countdown to Armageddon. But they don't understand the truth: the battle of Armageddon is being fought everywhere every day in the hearts and minds of all human beings. It's a spiritual war, not a physical one.

"For our struggle is not against flesh and blood," the apostle Paul declared, "but against the rulers, against the authorities, against the powers of this dark world and against the spiritual forces of evil in the heavenly realms" (Ephesians 6:12). This includes every agent of any level of power who is an instrument of evil.

Our battle is against spiritual forces, not physical ones. The devil holds great power. Even Jesus called him "the prince of this world" (John 12:31; 14:30; 16:11). Paul refers to him as "the ruler of the kingdom of the air" and "the spirit who is now at work in those who are disobedient" (Ephesians 2:2). Air is invisible, and yet it completely surrounds us. That's how Satan works. He is a subtle and unseen evil, battling the good purposes of God. He takes advantage of every human weakness to enslave men: pride, lust, greed, fear—even laziness. He uses error and false teaching to separate men from the true way of salvation—redemption through the blood of Christ. But the blood of Christ will always overcome the power Satan has over those who trust in Christ (Hebrews 2:14, 15; Revelation 12:10, 11).

> *The battle of Armageddon is being fought everywhere every day in the hearts and minds of all human beings.*

Christ's kingdom cannot be expanded by military conquest (John 18:36). Admittedly, God can intervene in the outcome of wars to cause conditions favorable to the spread of the gospel. But ultimately, the saving blood of the crucified Christ must be preached in order for people to be won for the Lord (Revelation 12:11). The real arena for this war with eternal consequences is the mind or heart. The human spirit is the battleground of ideas and doctrines, of righteousness and evil, of God and Satan. *This* is the battle of Armageddon.

The Book of Revelation is the story of war—the

eternal struggle between Satan and Christ for your soul—for the souls of all people. The story is told over and over again in Revelation, each time using powerful-but-different visual images. It's a cycle, going round and round, taking us ever closer to the last word of the battle. Jesus Christ will be victorious for those who love and follow him. The war has already been won. All you have to do is choose the side on which you want to fight to the death . . . or life.

Mount Megiddo

In three sections of Revelation, a great universal battle between the forces of evil and the army of God is described (Revelation 16:13-16; 19:11-21; 20:7-10). In Revelation 16:16 John says the place of battle is called Armageddon. The actual Hebrew term is *Har-Megiddo*, meaning "the mountain of Megiddo."

Mount Megiddo was the scene of many decisive battles. In the fifteenth century before Christ, the Egyptians defeated a combined army of Canaanites and Hittites there. The Israelites won a splendid victory over the Canaanites there in the thirteenth century B.C. In the seventh century before Christ, King Josiah was slain in an ill-fated battle at Megiddo against the forces of Pharaoh Necho. Even as late as World War I, the British general, Lord Allenby, won a battle against the Turks there.

Megiddo is located at the mouth of the great valley of Esdraelon where a narrow pass runs between the ridge of Mount Carmel on the north and the mountains of Samaria on the south. Invading armies from the north, south, or east had to pass Megiddo on their way to Egypt, Syria, or Babylon. Solomon stationed his cavalry at Megiddo to protect the kingdom of Israel, because a comparatively small force could hold off a much larger army by controlling the narrow pass. Of course, it entailed fierce hand-to-hand combat with heavy losses on both sides.

A classic historical example of holding a pass against overwhelming odds is Thermopylae, where 300 Spartans led by Leonidas held off the million-strong army of the Persians until the Greek city-states had time to muster their forces. The results were strategically decisive, but all of the 300 Spartans lost their lives in the terrible fighting which saved Greece and changed the history of the world.

A "battle at the pass" has become a standard expression to describe an all-out conflict whose outcome is decisive. And that is exactly why the term Armageddon is used by the Spirit in Revelation 16. It is not used to identify a geographic battle site or to imply a literal military campaign. This unreasonable interpretation was held by very few until the twentieth century. Let us examine some of the symbols.

The Opposing Armies

Two opposing armies face off on Mount Megiddo. On one side is Christ and his heavenly armies, clothed in white. On the other side is the devil and his earthly forces, who are called "the nations in the four corners of the earth, Gog and Magog"[1] (Revelation 20:8) and "the kings of the earth and the whole world" (16:14). Christ's army are the saints. Their

---

[1]Gog and Magog: These names are taken from Ezekiel 38:2, 3. Gog is identified there as the chief prince of Meshech and Tubal, and Magog is his land.

robes are white because they have washed them in the blood of the Lamb (Revelation 3:4, 5, 18; 6:11; 7:9, 13, 14). Those who follow the beast are those not registered in God's book of life. Those who follow the beast are the prime examples of idolatry. All people everywhere who are not Christians are simply lumped together as followers of the beast.

In the context of Revelation 16:13-16 and 20:8, 9, the distinction is between Christians and non-Christians. This reminds us of Jesus' statement in Matthew 12:30: "He who is not with me is against me, and he who does not gather with me scatters." There is no neutral ground in the battle of Armageddon. Everyone belongs to one side or the other. To do nothing is to take Satan's side by default. If you are not on Christ's side, you are automatically a part of Gog and Magog.

Difficulties with a Literal Interpretation of the Battle of Armageddon

Revelation 20 identifies the opposing sides in the great battle as Satan and his forces of evil (Gog and Magog) facing Christ and his army of good. Besides Gog and Magog, other nations mentioned in the war in Ezekiel 38 are Persia, Cush, Put, Gomer, and Beth (House of) Togarmah. All of these names are taken from the descendants of Japheth and Ham in Genesis 10, except Persia (listed as "Madai," or the Medes). All of them were powerful nations in ancient times but are no longer military powers, except Persia (now Iran) and Put (now Libya), which are third-rank powers today.

Until the break up of the Soviet Union, people expecting final world conflict to happen soon were most interested in Togarmah (now Armenia) because Ezekiel 38:6 says its troops will come from "the far

north." Since Armenia was one of the Russian repub-
lics to the far north of Israel, an attack upon Israel
by the Soviets was predicted. The attention of these
"prophets" will probably now switch to Communist
China.

But the precise identity of these ancient kingdoms
does not matter. At one time or another they were
threats to the kingdom of Israel, and they are listed
here only to create the image of a world conflict in
which _spiritual_ Israel (the church—Christ and his
forces) will always be badly outnumbered by people
of the carnal and materialistic world (Satan and his
forces).

_Do not despair at the odds you
face. You are sure of victory because the Supreme Power of the
universe is your leader._

The purpose of Ezekiel 38–39 and Revelation 16 is
summed up in Revelation 17:14—"They will make
war against the Lamb, but the Lamb will overcome
them because he is Lord of lords and King of kings—
and with him will be his called, chosen and faithful
followers." It is a message of assurance to a church
under siege: Do not despair at the odds you face. You
are sure of victory because the Supreme Power of the
universe is your leader.

The Battlefield

People who take Revelation literally say that the
last great battle will _physically_ take place at Mount
Megiddo. In ancient times a site such as Megiddo
could be the deciding factor of a battle. A small army

could face a huge enemy army in the pass and stop
its progress. As long as soldiers fought on the ground
with hand weapons, that was true. But it's no longer
true in our modern world of complex, powerful
airborne weaponry. A military force on Megiddo
today could be reduced to ashes by one nuclear
warhead. It would, in fact, be a deathtrap in a war of
supersonic aircraft and even faster rockets.

It is ridiculous to think that a world divided into
two military camps would confine its battlefield to
the tiny state of Israel, much less to the site of
Megiddo!

The Weapons

Gog and Magog are specifically named as the chief
warriors of the evil forces in both Revelation 20 and
Ezekiel 38 and 39. The battle described in the two
passages is clearly the same. Although the weapons
used are not mentioned in Revelation 20, they are in
Ezekiel: large and small shields, swords, helmets
(38:4, 5), bows and arrows (39:3), war clubs, and
spears (39:9). It says that the wood in the weapons
will serve as firewood for the Israelites for seven
years.

We are faced with two choices: either these prophetic sections of Ezekiel and Revelation are using
figurative language to teach a spiritual truth, or we
must believe that the world will revert to a primitive
society without computer technology, thermonuclear
rockets, airplanes, and firearms—a society where
warfare is waged by a cavalry (Ezekiel 38:15) armed
only with crude hand weapons. If we adopt a literal
interpretation, the citizens of Israel will no longer be
using electricity and petroleum products for fuel.
They will be using firewood gathered in the fields
and cut in the forests (which no longer exist in

Israel) until they are provided with the wooden weapons of Gog's army (Ezekiel 39:10).

Christians further the cause of Christ by wielding the "sword of the Spirit."

Satan himself relies upon spiritual weapons, upon deceit and distortion of truth. After all, Satan has founded many more religions than has Jesus Christ. This is illustrated in the introduction to the battle of Armageddon (16:13, 14). The effective weapons which build up Satan's forces are symbolized by the frogs coming out of the mouths of the dragon, the beast, and the false prophet. Since the frog was unclean to the Jews, it is a symbol for impure teachings. John identifies the dragon, beast, and false prophet as three evil spirits. So, the two concepts combined simply mean unholy spiritual teachings from three main sources. The beast would, no doubt, stand for wrong teachings of the false church. Some scholars suggest that the false prophet is Mohammed. The dragon may simply stand for all the idolatrous religions that cannot be included under Islam or perverted Christianity. Precise identification is not necessary or, perhaps, even possible. Here's the important point: Christians further the cause of Christ by wielding the "sword of the Spirit, which is the word of God" (Ephesians 6:17); Satan promotes his kingdom by false religious teaching.

The weapon the Lord uses is indeed a sword, but it's a different kind of sword. It comes out of his mouth (Revelation 19:15)—it is the word of God. And the weapon Satan uses comes from _his_ mouth. But he promotes his kingdom by _false_ religious teaching.

The battle of Armageddon is a war of ideas and spiritual values. The "battle of the pass" is waged every day in each person's heart, and the outcome is either a complete victory or an eternal defeat.

> *The human heart is a battlefield.*
> *We fight the battle of Armageddon*
> *every day as human beings.*

Some people take the prophecies of Armageddon literally and do not accept Christians as the armies following the Lamb. They believe that the "armies of heaven" are legions of angels. But consider this: if one angel could destroy Jerusalem by simply stretching out his hand (2 Samuel 24:16), or one angel could slay 185,000 Assyrians in a single night (2 Kings 19:35), what kind of contest would it be between armies of angels and the pitiful forces of Gog armed with spears and clubs? A battle waged between spiritual beings of unimagined power and a horde of bronze-age human beings goes beyond the limits of belief. It's simply illogical and unacceptable.

What the Battle of Armageddon Means to Christians

The human heart is a battlefield. We fight the battle of Armageddon every day as human beings. The enemy we oppose has many faces—people, material things, worldly systems. Behind every obstacle in our path is the masked face of Satan himself. His attacks upon us are constant and vicious. Five times in the letters to the seven churches, Jesus warned that the devil was behind the stress being endured by people. His power is great—but not overpowering. In the words of the prophet Elisha, "Those who are with us [the forces of good] are more than those who are with them [the forces of evil]" (2 Kings 6:16). The Lord's "chariots of fire" always surround you. We are certain of victory over Satan if we follow the Lamb by whose blood Satan is bound forever. The outcome of the battle between Christ and Satan is absolutely certain.

We are certain of victory over Satan if we follow the Lamb by whose blood Satan is bound forever.

Our concern should not be of some cosmic explosion. After all, physical death is not the ultimate terror. Jesus told us, "Do not be afraid of those who kill the body but cannot kill the soul" (Matthew 10:28). Death of the body is simply a necessary transition to our eternal state and has no lasting consequence for Christians. Jesus assured us that, "He who believes in me will live, even though he dies, and whoever lives and believes in me will never die" (John 11:25, 26). One of the ways the devil enslaves people is through their fear of physical death (Hebrews 2:14, 15).

Since the establishment of the modern state of Israel in 1948, there has been wide speculation that the battle of Armageddon is about to begin. Any new conflict that breaks out, particularly in the Middle East, increases worry and spawns wild stories that the end times are here. Christians do not need to be concerned with these latter-day prophecies. The

Lord said a long time ago, "You will hear of wars and rumors of wars, but see to it that you are not alarmed. Such things must happen, but the end is still to come" (Matthew 24:6).

> *We are both the warrior and the place of war. But we can be happy—the victory has already been won, and we're on the winning side!*

To win the battle of Armageddon, we must make Christ the Lord and leader of our hearts and minds. He will defeat the enemy for us if we follow him confidently through the fray. But we cannot be bystanders to the fight. We are in the fight because the fight is in us. We are both the warrior and the place of war. But we can be happy—the victory has already been won, and we're on the winning side!

Focusing Your Faith

1. When you think of the battle of Armageddon, what visual image is in your mind?

2. Where does the real battle of Armageddon take place? Can you feel the battle within you on a daily basis?

3. What would Christ, the Lord of heaven's armies, say to you about the battle of Armageddon?

4. Why can you laugh in the face of Satan when you think of this great battle?

5. "We are not bystanders to the fight. We are in the fight because the fight is in us." What does that statement mean to you personally?

6. As a Christian, what can your response be to the bad news we hear daily about battles Satan is winning—through drugs, divorce, politics, and even religion?

7. In the battle of Armageddon, on which side are you? How do you know?

Chapter Keys

beast symbolizes a power or institution—political or religious—which is hostile to God and his children.

crown symbolizes great honor or power.

dragon represents Satan.

fire symbolizes omniscience, sacrifice, or judgment.

lamb is the symbol for Christ—the sacrificial offering for sin.

sword is the symbol of aggressive power, whether good or bad.

white indicates great age when applied to hair; otherwise it symbolizes purity or sinlessness.

7 symbolizes salvation or the Savior. This use of seven is derived from four added to three—man (four) joined to God (three); man saved. Jesus himself is both God and man (a sum of seven again), and his mission of rejoining man to God is a sum of seven.

Chapter 2

The Seeds of War

The Red Dragon

Revelation 12:1-17

Key Message:

Satan desires to overthrow God's throne.

How did this great war begin anyway? Who planted the seeds of war? War is an *effect*. And, therefore it must necessarily have a *cause*. The reasons for conflict between two parties may be just or unjust. More likely, the root cause is injustice. The injustice may be real or perceived, but it is shown by one of the parties toward the other. Generally, a war arises from one party wanting something the other has, whether or not he has a legitimate claim to it: territory, wealth, power, access to markets, etc. In human affairs, as Jesus pointed out (Matthew 24:6), there will always be wars. There's not a single moment when war is not being waged in some part of the world. Conflict begins when somebody cannot get what he wants by peaceful means. "What causes fights and quarrels among you? Don't they come from your desires that battle within you? You want something but don't get it" (James 4:1, 2).

There is another war, though, that did not begin in time, nor was it caused by man. It's a cosmic war that began before the universe was created—an all-out war with God and his angels against Satan and his angels, a constant conflict between good and evil. Much about this war is beyond human understanding, and God has not chosen to reveal more than a few shadowy references to this ancient battle which will rage until the final judgment.

The devil rebelled over the question of authority.

As students of the Bible, we are like someone who enters the theater during the second act. He understands to a degree what is currently going on, but he can only vaguely suppose what must have happened in the first act. We are introduced to the devil in the form of a serpent in Genesis 3, but why he's in the garden or why he plots to harm man we are not told.

Before identifying the woman and child of Revelation 12:1-6, we'll explore verses 7-12. This passage gives us only a brief glimpse of the background of what is now happening on earth: *"And there was war in heaven. Michael and his angels fought against the dragon, and the dragon and his angels fought back. But he was not strong enough, and they lost their place in heaven. The great dragon was hurled down—that ancient serpent called the devil, or Satan, who leads the whole world astray. He was*

*hurled to the earth, and his angels with him. . . . But
woe to the earth and the sea, because the devil has
gone down to you! He is filled with fury, because he
knows that his time is short."*

So we know what he is doing on earth in Genesis
3—he had been thrown down there. We may infer
from Jude 6 (if the angels referred to were led by
Satan) that the devil rebelled over the question of
authority and that he persuaded some angels to join
his cause. This is our first evidence of the seeds of
Satan's war against God.

Michael, who led the battle against Satan's angels,
is identified in Daniel 12:1 as "the great prince who
protects your [God's] people." Jude 9 indicates that,
although an archangel, Michael obviously does not
outrank Satan.

There is an obscure reference in the lament over
the king of Tyre (Ezekiel 28:11-17) which does not
seem to fit any human king. Many scholars believe
that God is addressing Satan directly as the real
power behind the king of Tyre. It is said of him
that . . .

- he was a model of perfection, full of
  wisdom and perfect in beauty;

- he was in the garden of Eden;

- he was anointed to be one of the guard-
  ian cherubims (before God's throne);

- he was on God's holy mount until wickedness was found in him;

- he was expelled from the mount of God
  and thrown down to earth;

- his sin was pride.

If this is, indeed, a description of Satan, then he
had belonged to the very highest rank of heavenly

beings, standing in the presence of God himself. Job 1:6 refers to Satan as one of the "sons of God."

Satan still wields awesome power, but his doom is certain.

Jesus came to an earth where Satan had seized control (John 12:31; 14:30; 16:11). He diminished Satan's power by his crucifixion and resurrection, and he will finally destroy it completely when he raises all of the saints to eternal life (1 Corinthians 15:25, 26). It is this critical time between Christ's resurrection and the resurrection of the dead in Christ that is the focus of the battle of Armageddon, a battle into which all of us have been placed. Satan still wields awesome power (1 Peter 5:8), but his doom is certain.

For the limited time he has left, he is making every effort to steal away as many of God's people as he can. But just as Satan had planted his seeds of destruction before earthly time, God predestined a seed of salvation through a chosen people, the Jewish nation.

The Chosen Soil

Like other nations he had selected for special purposes, the Jews had one specific, holy assignment—to provide a pure race through whom God could send his Son into the world. He chose them for that particular task, and in that way they were his "chosen people." They were the chosen soil for the seed of Abraham, the son of David, and the army who would oppose Satan's evil forces. He even gave them a special law to help keep them pure and holy—fit for the seed of a King. However, like other nations he had chosen for other tasks, when their special purpose had been accomplished, the Jews returned to equal status with all other nations. Unfortunately, neither the Jews nor many others have accepted that "back-to-equal" status, even today.

The Bible is the record of God's working with the Jews to help them accomplish their divine purpose. In the Bible, God has clearly chosen the story of the Jews to dominate that of any other people.

Today, with our 20-20 hindsight, we often look back at the Jews and criticize their shortsightedness. "After centuries of waiting and watching for the Messiah, they didn't even recognize him when he came!" we say, shaking our heads in disbelief. Recognizing the biblical (and many modern) Jews' continued belief that they were and are the exclusive "chosen people of God," and annoyed by the "better-than-you" implications of their attitudes, our rearview image of them is often distorted. The role of the Jewish nation in God's eternal plan is often misunderstood.

For the limited time he has left, he is making every effort to steal away as many of God's people as he can.

The truth is, God's master plan was not spoiled, even though most of the Jews did not accept Jesus as the Messiah (Romans 9:6). Neither was the church a stopgap arrangement to cover God's "mistake" about the Jewish reaction to Jesus' preaching about the kingdom. God is perfect in every aspect of his Being; he does not and cannot make mistakes. He came as Jesus at exactly the right time (Galatians 4:4). He knew very well that physical Israel would reject him (Isaiah 53:3). The Jewish nation did fulfill its great universal mission. And it is their mission which is boldly pictured in Revelation 12—a mission which results in our salvation!

The Woman Clothed with the Sun

"A great and wondrous sign appeared in heaven: a woman clothed with the sun, with the moon under her feet and a crown of twelve stars on her head" (vs. 1).

There has been much speculation over the identity of the woman in this passage. Some students of Revelation believe that she is the church for this reason: Light is used as a symbol for truth. There are greater and lesser lights—the sun and the moon. The sources of spiritual light are the Old and New Testaments—the church is based upon the Old Testament prophecies but is clothed with the New Testament, or the gospel.

The problem with this concept is this: the woman of the sign gave birth to a son who would rule all the nations with an iron scepter. That son, according to Psalm 2:9, is the Son of God. But the church didn't produce the Christ; Christ produced the church. So, how can the woman be the church?

Others believe the woman is the Virgin Mary since she gave birth to the Christ child. That idea does not correspond, though, to what is asserted about the woman later on in the chapter.

The symbol of the woman probably stands for Judaism. Israel's very identity as a people was based upon the covenant made at Mount Sinai. So, her relationship to the Law is shown by the moon under her feet. The moon is a lesser light than the sun, just as the old law was a pale shadow compared to the brilliance of the gospel. The woman is clothed with the sun, that is, the brighter, more glorious gospel. Some people have said that the gospel, or new covenant, better befits the church than it does Judaism. But the gospel was first preached by Jews to Jews; so the early fellowship of Christians was entirely made up of Jews.

> *... Judaism gave the Christ, in the physical person of Jesus, to the world to stand against Satan's destructive army.*

The woman wears a crown of twelve stars which stand for the apostles. Judaism's crowning moment was the revelation of God's eternal plan of redemption to the world by Jewish preachers. The Jews were preserved as a chosen people by God for one glorious purpose—to bring forth the Messiah into the world and to be the first to proclaim salvation through his blood to all people.

The obvious purpose of this woman, then, was to bring forth the male child who would rule all nations. In other words, Judaism gave the Christ, in the physical person of Jesus, to the world to stand against Satan's destructive army.

The Red Dragon

"Then another sign appeared in heaven: an enormous red dragon with seven heads and ten horns and

seven crowns on his heads," (vs. 3).

The great red dragon with seven heads[1] and ten horns represents Satan and the agents he would use to fight the church. It also stands for the heathen world kingdom and what grew out of it—the great falling away from the faith. The image from verse 4 of the dragon's tail sweeping away a third of the stars shows Satan's breaking up of a powerful human system with prominent leaders. In this case, no doubt, it means Judaism with its priesthood and established institutions (compare Daniel 8:10).

The Jewish system was sometimes sporadically persecuted and weakened by the Roman Empire. But during the critical early period of the birth and spread of Christianity, Judaism was favored by the Roman government. In fact, the Jews were allowed to practice their religion freely.

The latter part of verse 4 shows Satan's evil plot to thwart God's saving plan in its initial stages. "The dragon stood in front of the woman who was about to give birth, so that he might devour her child the moment it was born." Indeed the devil made three dramatic attempts to destroy Christ's mission on earth: (1) He used Herod in an attempt to kill the newborn Jesus; (2) he tempted Jesus in the wilderness and actually asked Jesus to worship him; (3) he physically murdered Jesus on the cross. His failure to understand the effects of the crucifixion is noted by Paul in 1 Corinthians 2:8: "None of the rulers of

---

[1]The use of seven in connection with the devil seems a contradiction since seven is the number of salvation. The devil is a usurper, promising what he cannot deliver. He masquerades as an angel of light, promising the salvation he cannot deliver.

this age understood it, for if they had, they would not have crucified the Lord of glory."

Satan probably would have succeeded in his attempt to kill the infant Jesus if God had not helped directly, sending an angel to warn Joseph in a dream. In the sense that he was protected by God's providence, the "child was snatched up to God and to his throne" (vs. 5).

God's Ongoing Purpose for the Jews

Verse 6 has caused many questions about God's ongoing purpose for Jews. For instance, why would God prepare a place for the Jews and take care of them if he does not have some ultimate purpose for them?

The special privilege the Roman government gave the Jews to freely practice their faith was necessary for the early church to survive. Herod the Great and his father Antipater secured this preferred treatment for the Jewish religion through astute politics. So the Christians were not persecuted by official Rome until after the temple was destroyed in A.D. 70, and the Jewish religion was banned. During this early period, persecution of the church originated with the Jews themselves, not from Rome.

The Roman government simply regarded Christians as another division of Judaism—"the sect of the Nazarene." They dismissed the Jews' hatred of Christians as a sort of family squabble between Jewish groups disagreeing over their own law. That explains Gallio's offhand dismissal of the charges against Paul (Acts 18:14, 15): "If you Jews were making a complaint about some misdemeanor or serious crime, it would be reasonable for me to listen to you. But since it involves questions about words and names of your own law—settle the matter yourselves. I will not be a judge of such things."

So much is clear: the infant church grew and spread in the shadow of Judaism until it no longer needed that protection. But after the Jews had served God's purposes in bringing Christ and salvation to the whole world, why did God continue to protect them as a people? That's what verse 6 seems to be saying: "The woman fled into the desert to a place prepared for her by God, where she might be taken care of for 1,260 days."

The most obvious meaning of this verse is the deportation of Palestinian Jews and their scattering throughout the world after the Jewish Roman war of A.D. 66-70. "Desert" (or wilderness) is a symbol for the pagan world (see Isaiah 35:1, 6). The 1,260 days is a symbolic number. Elsewhere it is referred to as 42 months, or 3 1/2 years. It does not represent a time period, but a concept. These figures are used to represent a span of 3 1/2 years which is half of 7— the salvation number. Probably, it indicates that Judaism will continue as a religious-ethical group, but without salvation or a savior. The question is, why? Any explanation based on God's favoring the Jews as a separate people is not workable. (More information on this question is detailed in the Why Will Judaism Continue? section at the end of this chapter.)

The Dragon Turns His Rage

Satan realized at the resurrection that he had lost the war with God. So, he was determined to use the time he had left to wreak as much destruction as he could. Because the woman (Judaism) birthed the male child (the church), he first directed his fury against the Jews. These attacks included the destruction of Jerusalem under Titus, the later Bar-Kokhba rebellion[2] and every attempt to annihilate the Jews, including Hitler's holocaust. He never succeeded in destroying them though. That's because God had ordained that there would always be Gentile countries who would give them shelter. Satan finally saw that he could never succeed in destroying the Jewish people (which in the second quarter of the first century included Jewish Christians). So he turned his rage on their offspring, the church—"those who obey God's commandments and hold to the testimony of Jesus" (12:17).

The chapter ends by saying "the dragon stood on the shore of the sea." This possibly means that Satan has now turned his rage on the Gentile world (sea) where the church is centered. We are now the ones facing the red dragon and feeling his rage.

[2]Bar-Kokhba (Son of the Star) was a false Messiah who, at the beginning of the second century, led the Jews in a futile attempt to overcome the Romans. About one-half million Jews and an equal number of Romans were killed.

The following information has been included in this chapter for supplemental study.

Why Will Judaism Continue?

1. God makes no distinction between Jew and Gentile in the offer of his grace through Christ. "For there is no difference between Jew and Gentile—the same Lord is Lord of all and richly blesses all who call on him" (Romans 10:12).

2. The Jews' descent from Abraham does not secure for them any special privilege. "And do not think you can say to yourselves, 'We have Abraham as our father.' I tell you that out of these stones God can raise up children for Abraham" (Matthew 3:9). Also, "A man is not a Jew if he is only one outwardly, nor is circumcision merely outward and physical. No, a man is a Jew if he is one inwardly; and circumcision is circumcision of the heart, by the Spirit, not by the written code" (Romans 2:28, 29).

3. An unconverted Jew is as condemned by God as the unconverted Gentile. Paul said, "What shall we conclude then? Are we [Jews] any better? Not at all! We have already made the charge that Jews and Gentiles alike are all under sin" (Romans 3:9).

4. Like every other person, a Jew can only be saved by accepting the gospel. "And if

they do not persist in unbelief, they will
be grafted in, for God is able to graft
them in again" (Romans 11:23). "We
believe it is through the grace of our
Lord Jesus that we are saved, just as
they are" (Acts 15:11).

So, we Gentiles do not need to think that God has
made any "special deal" for the salvation of the Jews.
On the other hand, God does not put some roadblock
in the way of the Jews' conversion because their kin
shed the blood of Christ. God is not willing that a
single human being should perish (2 Peter 3:9)—
whether Jew or Gentile.

Still, the apostle Paul expressed the fervent hope,
that a time would come when the Jews would no
longer resist the gospel: ". . . I make much of my
ministry in the hope that I may somehow arouse my
own people to envy and save some of them. For if
their rejection is the reconciliation of the world,
what will their acceptance be but life from the
dead?" (Romans 11:13b-15). "Israel has experienced
a hardening in part until the full number of the
Gentiles has come in. And so all Israel will be saved,
as it is written: 'The deliverer will come from Zion;
he will turn godlessness away from Jacob. And this
is my covenant with them when I take away their
sins' " (Romans 11:25-27).

Much has been made of Paul's statement: "And so
all Israel will be saved." So, we need to look at two
grammatical points:

Step 1. *So* in verse 26 does not mean "therefore." The word in Greek is *houtos*,
which means "in this way," the way
Paul has already outlined—salvation
through faith in Christ.

Step 2. *All Israel* does not mean every physical

Jew. That would contradict the "some"
in Romans 11:14. If Paul had meant to
say that the entire Jewish nation will
be saved, he would have used *holos*
(entire) instead of *pas* for "all." "All
Israel" is comprehensive and includes
the "Israel" and the "Gentiles" mentioned in verse 25.

In other words, all of spiritual Israel, the church,
will be saved in exactly the same way—through the
grace of God by faith in Christ as his Son.

The Debt of Grace

Here are some important practical conclusions to
consider about the role of the Jewish nation:

1. Gentile Christians owe a debt of gratitude to
the Jewish people. After all, they were the nation
who gave us the Christ and, thus, salvation. As
God's instrument in working out his plan to
save men of all races, they suffered greatly at the
hands of our Gentile ancestors. Jewish tongues first
preached the gospel of eternal salvation, and many
of those faithful preachers paid with their lives.

Paul felt that Gentiles should feel some debt of
honor to the Jews: "For if the Gentiles have shared
in the Jews' spiritual blessings, they owe it to the
Jews to share with them their material blessings"
(Romans 15:27). Today, Paul might say, since the
Jews shared the gospel with us in the first century,
we owe it to them to return the favor in the twentieth and twenty-first centuries.

The Jews, as a whole, desperately need salvation
today. Do we, who are saved only because Jews
shared Christ with us, care that they are lost? Will

we take Christ to those who brought him to us?

2. God has made no special "deal" with the Jews to be saved in any way other than obedience to the gospel. Neither has he planned for them a special period of time that we Gentiles won't have as an opportunity to be saved. God does not love them more than he loves us, or vice versa.

3. God has not rejected the Jews because they crucified the Christ. They, like all people, are lost because of sin—any sin, all sin—not some special guilt peculiar to their race. God wants them to accept his grace, which is freely offered to all.

Focusing Your Faith

1. Can you see God and Satan making strategic moves with nations and rulers in today's world? Describe what you see.

2. In the last 25 years, do you think Satan or God has claimed more victories? Why?

3. As Christians, how should we feel about the Jewish people today? Why?

4. List the three dramatic attempts Satan made to ruin Christ's mission to earth.

5. What is the irony of Satan's evil plot to kill Jesus on the cross?

6. As a soldier of the cross, how can you personally defeat the Red Dragon in your life?

7. What would you tell your child if she came to you in the middle of the night afraid of the devil? Why?

Chapter Key

beast symbolizes a power or institution—political or religious—which is hostile to God and his children.

chain denotes a binding or restricting power.

dragon represents Satan.

key represents authority. The person with the key had power over the house or kingdom to open or close the door.

throne represents authority.

1,000 represents absolute perfection—ten times ten times ten is one thousand, completeness infused with divinity.

Chapter 3

The Conflict
Is Between Kingdoms
The 1,000-Year Reign

∽

Revelation 20:1-10

The holy war that rages in the world is between two opposing kingdoms—the kingdom of light and the kingdom of darkness. Jesus, the Light of the world, leads the armies of good. Satan, the Prince of darkness, directs the armies of evil. And they are in mortal battle—the battle of Armageddon—for your soul.

> **Key Message:**
>
> *This is not a period in time but a spiritual kingdom where God dwells with his people today.*

There is no doubt that the forces of Satan will bring strong pressures to bear against God's "camp" and "city" (the church). But Christians will certainly not be destroyed. We will be rescued, not by our own power, but by divine intervention. The conflict between Christ's kingdom and Satan's kingdom will end with Satan's complete destruction in the fires of hell, together with all those who have served him.

Christians will be victorious through the blood of the Lamb and will reign with him forever.

The Messenger, the Key, and the Chain

"And I saw an angel coming down out of heaven, having the key to the Abyss and holding in his hand a great chain. He seized the dragon, that ancient serpent, who is the devil, or Satan, and bound him for a thousand years" (Revelation 20:1, 2).

The mighty messenger (angel) who comes down from heaven with the divine order to bind Satan cannot be anyone except Christ himself.

A key symbolizes authority—in this case, it's the authority to open and shut, bind and free. Revelation 3:7 tells us that Jesus is the one who has the key of David, the key to the kingdom of God's people. Isaiah 22:22 says that the coming Messiah would carry the key of the house of David on his shoulder (that is, the cross), with the power to open and shut the door of the kingdom. So Revelation 20:1 is identifying Jesus as the messenger with the power to admit and exclude from God's kingdom. Jesus says, "I hold the keys of death and Hades" (1:18).

A chain is a symbol of binding or restriction. Since the devil is a spirit, he could not be bound with a material chain. There is, however, a very powerful force which can bind Satan and forbid him entry to the kingdom of God. John tells us that this binding force is the blood of the Lamb and the gospel message (12:10, 11). Through his death on the cross, Jesus destroyed Satan's power to rule men through sin, if they accept the gospel. Therefore, chapter 20 portrays the first coming of Jesus to earth to shed his blood to buy men back from the power of Satan. The Cross sets men free, but it binds Satan.

The Thousand Years

"He seized the dragon, that ancient serpent, who is the devil, or Satan, and bound him for a thousand years" (20:2).

One thousand is one of several mystic numbers that had symbolic meaning for the Hebrews. Even before the Christian age began, this symbol was used by Jewish and Gentile writers in referring to a coming "golden age."

The 1,000-year symbol was a concept understood by both Jewish and Gentile believers. They understood it to mean the "golden age" or "the age of the Messiah." The new Jerusalem is also described as a cube whose length, breadth, and height are equal (21:16). Any informed Jewish Christian would quickly see the parallel to the holy of holies—God's dwelling place.

_____

The 1,000 years ... is God's reign in the lives of men.

_____

The 1,000 years, then, is not to be understood as an earthly calendar period. It is, instead, a symbol for that sphere in which God dwells with his people. It is God's reign in the lives of men. It's that time when God is present with and in his chosen people, his kingdom. Satan cannot harm these people because he is bound with that great chain, the shed blood of Jesus.

"He threw him into the Abyss, and locked and sealed it over him, to keep him from deceiving the nations anymore until the thousand years were ended" (20:3). The "abyss" is what the King James

Version called the "bottomless pit." It's probably the same as the "gloomy dungeons" of 2 Peter 2:4 and the "darkness" and "everlasting chains" of Jude 6 into which rebellious angels were cast. All these descriptions are physical images which our human minds can grasp. They explain this spiritual truth: Satan's power has been broken over the redeemed! God's spirit of truth guards those from all nations who have come to Christ, leaving the error and darkness of the devil's influence.

The phrase "until the thousand years were ended" simply means that within God's kingdom Satan's power is broken. Outside the fortress of the kingdom, unprotected by the blood of Christ and the sealing of the Holy Spirit, Satan still has control over the world of men.

"After that, he must be set free for a short time." Again, time is used to symbolize spheres of spiritual relationships. The "short time" is not qualified; it simply means a limitation. It is short when compared to what existed before Christ's blood was shed. Once Satan ran wild in the lives of all men, but now he is restricted from those in Christ. His being "set free" describes the power Satan still has outside that special area or fortress protected by Christ's blood. Satan still uses the ugly power of sin to destroy the souls of men who have no relationship to God through Christ.

Authority to Judge

"I saw thrones on which were seated those who had been given authority to judge" (20:4a). Jesus promised his apostles that in the new birth (John 3:3-5; Titus 3:5; 1 Peter 1:23) they would reign with him and judge the twelve tribes of Israel (Matthew 19:28). The twelve actual tribes of Israel obviously

cannot be meant, since ten of those tribes had been totally lost since the eighth century B.C. They have, in fact, been absorbed into all the Semitic peoples of the Middle East. At most, only remnants of Judah, with a smattering of Benjamin and Levi, still exist in the bloodlines of the Jewish population today, which is, in any case, highly mixed with virtually all Gentile races. Jesus was, of course, referring to spiritual Israel—God's covenant people in the Christian age.

_____

*Overcoming sin in our daily lives
is occurring at the same time as
our sitting with Christ on the
throne.*

_____

The authority of the apostles remains intact today through the inspired Word, which they preached and recorded for us. The divine Word is the standard of judgment (John 12:48; Hebrews 4:12). Anyone who uses this apostolic Word to convict men of sin and move them to repentance is judging on Christ's behalf. Paul wrote in Ephesians 2:6 that "God raised us up with Christ and seated us with him in the heavenly realms in Christ Jesus." In Revelation 3:21 we are promised that all Christians who are "continuing to overcome" will be given the honor of sitting with Christ on his throne. That means that overcoming sin in our daily lives is occurring at the same time as our sitting with Christ on the throne.

Being given the authority to judge simply means that Christians apply the instrument of judgment—the inspired Word of God. It does not mean that we have the ability and wisdom to sit in judgment over others. God's Word makes the judgments—our responsibility is to be faithful to its standards.

The Beheaded

"And I saw the souls of those who had been be-headed because of their testimony for Jesus and because of the word of God" (vs. 4).

This statement has been interpreted by some to refer to those who are physically put to death for preaching the gospel (the martyrs). They say these martyrs do not go to an intermediate state (Para-dise) in between earthly life and heaven. Instead, they go immediately to live with God and Christ. There they will reign with Christ until the second resurrection, at which time they will be joined by their brethren who were not martyred. It is inconsis-tent to take this verse so literally in a section that is otherwise so rich in symbolism. The original Greek here identifies those who were beheaded as the same persons who did not worship the beast. This descrip-tion fits all true Christians.

Those beheaded are those who surrendered their will to God and "died" to their former worldly life.

In any case, if the passage is taken literally, it does not include *all* the martyrs—only the ones beheaded. Those who were martyred by being cruci-fied or torn to pieces in the arena by wild beasts would be excluded from sitting with Christ. "Be-headed" must, therefore, have a symbolic meaning. Paul alludes to this death in 2 Timothy 2:11, 12: "Here is a trustworthy saying: If we died with him,

we shall also live with him; if we endure, we will
also reign with him." Those beheaded are those who
surrendered their will to God and "died" to their
former worldly life. They became new creations in
Jesus Christ, having experienced a new birth, having taken on a new name and a new lifestyle, they
are forever dead to the world out of which they have
come. They gave up direction of their lives, making
Christ their Lord, or "head" (Ephesians 5:23, 24).

"They had not worshiped the beast or his image
and had not received his mark on their foreheads or
their hands" (vs. 4b). Those who were beheaded (that
is, died to the world) had nothing to do with the
beast (Satan). They were neither believers in him
(marked on their foreheads) or his servants (marked
on their hands).

The First Resurrection

_"They came to life and reigned with Christ a
thousand years. (The rest of the dead did not come to
life until the thousand years were ended.) This is the
first resurrection. Blessed and holy are those who
have part in the first resurrection. The second death
has no power over them, but they will be priests of
God and of Christ and will reign with him a thousand years"_ (vss. 4c-6).

Those who die to the world come back to life in
Christ's kingdom (symbolized as "the thousand
years"), which is the church. They, and they only,
will live in Christ's kingdom. _All_ people were dead in
sin (Ephesians 2:1, 2), but some have been raised to
sit with Christ (Ephesians 2:5, 6) by God's grace.
Unconverted sinners are spiritually dead and,
therefore, do not come to life in that realm where
Christ is Lord of men's lives. Paul expresses it this
way: "I have been crucified with Christ and I no

longer live, but Christ lives in me" (Galatians 2:20).

"The rest of the dead did not come to life until the thousand years were ended" (vs. 5a). This statement does not mean, as many have thought, that the rest of the dead (those separated from Christ) will live again at the end of the 1,000 years. It simply means that spiritual life in the kingdom of Christ is not available to those who have not died to the world. Remember that the 1,000 years is a symbol of the spiritual realm in which Christ dwells with his people. With that in mind, the statement means that in the entire fellowship of *true believers* there will not be even one follower of Satan. However, some of Satan's followers will infiltrate the physical church dressed as angels of light. But they will never be part of the *spiritual church* that gains life eternal.

... spiritual life in the kingdom of Christ is not available to those who have not died to the world.

"This is the first resurrection" (vs. 5b). Since this passage is dealing with spiritual life and spiritual death, the resurrection meant here is also spiritual. It, no doubt, refers to the symbolism pictured in baptism—of death and resurrection in union with Christ. Paul describes the spiritual significance of baptism by calling it a death, a burial, and a resurrection to a new life (Romans 6:1-4). This meaning is consistent with Jesus' teaching in John 3:3-5. These passages do not teach the sacramental value of water in freeing men from sin. Instead they describe baptism as a commitment of faith in dying to the world and accepting the Lordship of Jesus over the

penitent believer's life.

The Premillennial View

Probably no section of Scripture has caused more wild speculation and theories than Revelation 20:1-10. It is the basis for most of the beliefs about the second coming that are lumped together under the term *premillennialism.* This term simply means "before the 1,000 years." There are many variations in the specifics of premillennialism believed by different groups. But most of them share some or all of the following premises:

1. The 1,000-year reign will be a literal, earth-based kingdom in which Christ will reign over resurrected saints, other Christians, and Jews who are his willing servants. But he will also exercise power over all nations.

2. Christ will sit upon the actual throne of David in Jerusalem.

3. The devil will be excluded from this universal reign until the 1,000 years are completed. Then he will be freed to gather all the people who have not been converted to loyalty to Christ for a great battle against Christ and his army.

Many premillennialists believe that the 1,000-year reign will not begin immediately at Christ's coming. Rather, they say he will come first to receive the saved into a seven-year period of bliss somewhere away from the earth. They call this period of bliss "the rapture." During this seven years, they say the battle of Armageddon (see chapter 1 of this book) will result in a victory of Christ's angelic armies over the earthly forces of Satan. A cleansing of the earth will take place in preparation for Christ's return to earth with all his saints to begin his 1,000-year reign. During this same time, Satan will be bound in a bottomless pit. Armageddon supposedly will take place between the 1,000-year reign and the final judgment during a brief period (the "little season") when Satan is again freed to lead the evil nations.

While people who believe the premillennial view are obviously sincere and convinced of their belief, the Bible, when carefully examined, does not support their doctrine.

The Millennium and Me

Whatever the system of millennialism—and there are many—all are based upon Revelation 20:1-7. But, consider these facts, which are *essential* to such doctrines, that are *not* found in these verses:

1. *An earthly reign.* The text does not mention the location of the thrones.

2. *A kingdom at Jerusalem.* There is no mention of Jerusalem.

3. *A reign over actual Israelites.* The text mentions martyrs, not Jews.

Revelation 20:1-10 has a marvelous, positive message of reassurance for the church under persecution, in whatever age or whatever guise that persecution may take. But, it is *not* a description of Christ's future reign on David's throne in Jerusalem.

The 1,000-year reign is the spiritual reign of Christ in the hearts and lives of Christians. Because we are his instruments for growth in the kingdom, we reign with Christ by preaching and living the gospel. Only those of us who have died to the world and have been raised to a new life are safe in the fortress of the "thousand years." Only there are we protected from the forces of Satan by the blood of Christ and the power of the Word. The rest of mankind is not spiritually alive. In their lives, Satan has not been bound by the great chain of Christ's blood.

He still holds them under his deceitful spell and uses them to persecute Christ's people.

> ## *The 1,000-year reign is the spiritual reign of Christ in the hearts and lives of Christians.*

Still, God's power will rescue his chosen ones from Satan's evil plot to destroy the church. And the devil and his agents will finally be thrown into hell. The war between the two kingdoms goes on, but the kingdom of Christ will win the war. Praise God for his unspeakable gift!

54

Haven't You Heard? There's a WAR Going On! _____

Focusing Your Faith

1. Since you've been under the protection of the blood of Christ, has Satan's power been diminished in your life?

2. Paint a word picture of the 1,000-year reign.

3. What sounds of war can be heard from the kingdom of God? From the kingdom of Satan?

4. How does it make you feel to know that all true believers have been beheaded for the cause of Christ? (See The Beheaded, in this chapter.)

5. Why is it important today for Christians to see that outside of the reign of Christ, Satan is as powerful as he's ever been?

6. Who is included in the first resurrection?

7. When Christ returns, will the 1,000-year reign begin or end? Why do you think so?

Chapter Keys

lamb   is the symbol for Christ—the sacrificial offering for sin.

living creature
           represents the Holy Spirit. "Creature" is a bad translation in the context; "being" is preferable.

throne   represents authority.

white   indicates great age when applied to hair; otherwise it symbolizes purity or sinlessness.

4   is the number of the earth or the material universe.

12   is the number of concrete completeness— everyone or everything present and accounted for.

12,000   is all the saved of one tribe. Twelve (from the analogy of the twelve tribes) is the equivalent of saying "everybody." The 1,000 is the messianic kingdom—the saved. Therefore, all the saved of one tribe is 12,000; the saved of all 12 tribes (i.e., every nation or race) would be 144,000.

144,000   the saved; the church.

Chapter 4

The Lord's
Army

The 144,000

Revelation 7; 14

> **Key Message:**
>
> *The 144,000 represents all true believers who are engaged in the Lord's battle against evil.*

Each time a country goes to war, many patriotic citizens rush to enlist in the army. But not everyone will be selected for battle. Some are classified as 4 F, "unfit for the fighting forces." Rejected. Not allowed entry. Denied access.

In Revelation John tells of an exclusive army—one from which no one would wish to be rejected. It is the army of the 144,000.

This army of 144,000 represents the saved kingdom of Christ. And we've already learned that we're either in his kingdom or in the lost kingdom of the enemy—Satan. There's no middle ground.

The 144,000 "special soldiers" of Revelation 7 and 14 embody a mysterious, exciting, terrifying concept.

58

Haven't You Heard? There's a WAR Going On! _____

The "144,000" brings to mind all kinds of questions for the average person who takes Revelation literally.

- Am I in the army of 144,000?

- What about my mate and family?

- How can I know for sure if I'm in this relatively tiny number of chosen people, considering the billions of people who have lived?

- If I'm *not* in the 144,000, why even bother with this Christianity stuff? It's wasted effort!

- If I don't have a chance at eternal life, why not at least live it up now?

The great multitude of 144,000 soldiers is mysterious—if we are not sure who they are; exciting—if we're part of them; and terrifying—if we're *not* one of them. There are a variety of views held by futurists and literalists on the identity of the 144,000. (Additional information on this topic may be found at the end of this chapter.) So, how does this confusing concept fit into the victorious message of John's revelation?

Understanding the Symbol

"Then I saw another angel coming up from the east, having the seal of the living God. He called out in a loud voice to the four angels who had been given power to harm the land and the sea: 'Do not harm the land or the sea or the trees until we put a seal on the foreheads of the servants of our God.' Then I heard the number of those who were sealed: 144,000 from all the tribes of Israel" (Revelation 7:2-4).

"Then I looked, and there before me was the Lamb, standing on Mt. Zion, and with him 144,000 who

*had his name and his Father's name written on their
foreheads . . . and they sang a new song before the
throne and before the four living creatures and the
elders. No one could learn the song except the 144,000
who had been redeemed from the earth. . . . They
follow the Lamb wherever he goes. They were purchased from among men and offered as firstfruits to
God and the Lamb"* (14:1, 3, 4).

The number 144,000 can be derived from the use
of the Hebrew mystic numbers—12 x 12 x 1,000. To
the Hebrews twelve represented the number of
concrete completeness—everything or everyone
accounted for. This distinguishes it from the use of
ten as the number of *abstract* completeness—completeness of degree or quality. In the case of persons,
twelve stands for the whole group, or everybody
present. And quite probably, it comes from the
twelve sons of Jacob whose descendants were called
the twelve tribes of Israel. They were God's special
people of promise.

**The number 144,000 is the
symbolic total of the saved from
every nation.**

The number 1,000 is the ultimate degree of perfection and is the number of the kingdom, where God
dwells with his people.

The number 144,000, then, is 12 (everybody) times
12 (out of all the 12 tribes) times 1,000 (Christ's
kingdom). It is the symbolic total of the saved from
every nation. It is *not* meant to be understood as the
literal number of those who will be saved.

The Real 144,000

The 144,000, then, are those who follow Christ (Revelation 14:4); those who bear God's seal (7:4), which is the Holy Spirit (Ephesians 1:13; 4:30); those who are dressed in white robes washed in the blood of the Lamb (Revelation 7:14); those who serve God day and night in his temple (7:15). God's temple is the church, the spiritual body of Christ (Ephesians 1:22, 23). They no longer hunger spiritually, because the Lamb feeds them and gives them living water (Revelation 7:16, 17; Matthew 5:6; John 4:10, 14; 6:35).

You can know that you're one of the "144,000" saved and sanctified saints who will be honored for all eternity.

The army concept for Christ's followers is consistent with many New Testament scriptures which teach that Christians are engaged in a relentless, deadly war. Our warfare is not physical, and our weapons are not of this world (2 Corinthians 10:3, 4). Still, our weapons are extremely powerful and can demolish the strongholds of Satan, who leads the forces of darkness (Ephesians 6:12). Only those who fight the good fight of faith will grasp the eternal life to which we have been called (1 Timothy 6:12). Being a soldier of Christ Jesus may involve endurance of hardship and sacrifice of earthly things (2 Timothy 2:3, 4). Being a member of the Lord's army requires following him wherever he goes (Revelation 14:4)—a demanding commitment.

The "armies of heaven" in Revelation 19:14 are the identical followers of the Lamb found standing with him on Mt. Zion (14:1) and serving God in his temple (7:15). They are armies of heaven because they fight a spiritual war led by Christ, not an earthly army which wages physical war. The nature of the conflict in which the heavenly armies are engaged is indicated by their leader's weapon. A sword comes out of his mouth—it's a spoken message. The word of God is the sword of the Spirit (Ephesians 6:17), the living and active weapon of God which is sharper than any literal, two-edged sword (Hebrews 4:12).

Many commentators have believed that the "armies of heaven" of Revelation 19:14 refers to legions of angels. But that does not correspond to the nature of the warfare described. It's a war waged with the sword of Christ's mouth—the gospel. That gospel was not given to angels to preach; the gospel was placed "in jars of clay" (2 Corinthians 4:7). Human beings are, in fact, those "jars of clay" who live on earth to wage Christ's war.

The reference to the army's uniform—"fine linen, clean and bright"—also agrees with the description of the bride of the Lamb, the church in Revelation 19:8, and those whose robes have been washed in the blood of the Lamb (7:14).

The 144,000, therefore, symbolizes the saved, the church, who comprise the army of the Lord, clothed in his righteousness and readiness to follow him. If we can know that we're in his church, we can just as surely know that we're of the symbolic 144,000 saved and sanctified saints who will be honored for all eternity.

The Great Multitude
Revelation 7:4-15; 14:1

"Then I heard the number of those who were sealed: 144,000 from all the tribes of Israel . . ." (7:4).

"After this I looked and there before me was a great multitude that no one could count from every nation, tribe, people and language, standing before the throne" (7:9).

How does the special class of 144,000 relate to the crowd that no one could count? A prominent futurist teaching is that the 144,000 will be the total number of people taken up to heaven. And that the "great multitude" will remain on a renewed earth. Revelation, however, describes the 144,000 being sealed *on the earth*. And the great multitude is standing before the Lamb's throne (7:9).

So, if the passage is taken literally, we would have to make the *opposite* conclusion: the 144,000 were left on *earth*, and a numberless multitude are in heaven before the throne. But, the 144,000 and the great multitude are two names for the same people—all are the saved. John *heard* the number 144,000, but he *saw* the multitude that no man could number. They are "before the throne" because they serve and honor the Lamb.

The 144,000 and the great multitude are the same— all the saved.

Some have thought that the multitude is standing before God's throne in heaven, but the following description shows that they are on earth. They are serving him in his temple (7:15), which is the word used for the church (Greek *naos*, "shrine") or Christians (1 Corinthians 3:16, 17; 2 Corinthians 6:16; Ephesians 2:21). The "shrine" is the place where a deity meets with his worshipers. In Revelation 7:15 it is stated that the Lamb on the throne will "spread his tent over them."[1] The Lord is present with his followers in the church ("the tent"—_naos_), his spiritual body. But the church on earth is but a temporary dwelling, a tabernacle, until the close of the gospel age. It is a realized phase of his eternal kingdom but not the final state. Christ will come,

> *But in the present earthly phase of the kingdom "the dwelling of God is with men."*

and all Christians "will be caught up together with them in the clouds to meet the Lord in the air. And so will we be with the Lord forever" (1 Thessalonians 4:17). "The end will come, when he hands over the kingdom to God the Father after he has destroyed all dominion, authority and power. For he must reign until he has put all enemies under his feet. The last enemy to be destroyed is death" (1 Corinthians 15:24-26). But in the present, earthly phase of the kingdom "the dwelling of God is with men" (Revelation 21:3).

In Revelation 14:1 the Lamb stands with the 144,000 on Mount Zion. This generally has been

[1]The Greek word used for "spread his tent" is _skenoo_, the same word translated in John 1:14 as "made his dwelling among us." It literally means to "pitch a tent" and refers to a temporary dwelling. The noun form _skene_ is used six times in Hebrews for the Mosaic tabernacle and twice in reference to the church. In Hebrews 8:2 the church is called "the true tabernacle set up by the Lord, not by man" and "the greater and more perfect tabernacle that is not man-made" in Hebrews 9:11.

64

Haven't You Heard? There's a WAR Going On! _____

taken to mean they are in heaven, but that violates the prophetic use of Zion. Of the approximately 150 times the name Zion is used in the Old Testament, it always means either the literal Mt. Zion in Jerusalem, or else it refers to the age of Christ's kingdom,

---

There are no spectators allowed; every true Christian is a participant.

---

the church. It is never used to refer to heaven. Zion was the highest point in Jerusalem, and David's throne, from which he ruled all of the twelve tribes of Israel, was there. So the prophets used Zion as a symbol for God's rule over all his people through the messianic King of David's house, Jesus Christ.

The Army Is Christ's True Followers

When we accept God's gift of salvation, we automatically accept his commission to engage in spiritual warfare against Satan's army. Our commission is an ongoing commitment to oppose the Evil One as we use the armor of God to deflect his fiery darts of temptation. God has called us into a daily battle against Satan and his forces of evil. There are no spectators allowed; every true Christian is a participant. With the spiritual sword of the gospel in our hands, we can confidently battle the forces of evil. Satan's a terrifying enemy, but we can look ahead in the battle to the great Conqueror on his white horse. He is blazing a trail through the enemy lines for us. Only those who continue to press forward will win the victor's crown of life.

The following information has been included in this chapter for supplemental study. See also Appendix 3, The Measuring Rod and the Two Witnesses, in the back of this book.

Varying Views

Views vary widely on the idea of the 144,000. One view is that God has a special destiny reserved for the physical descendants of Abraham (literal, Israel). The view that God will show special favor to the Jews does not agree with the Scriptures. God's Word consistently teaches that there is no favoritism of persons with him. This mistaken view even influences foreign policies of Western governments. Various Protestant groups pressure the State Department to give preferred treatment to the state of Israel over Arab countries. Otherwise, they believe they are opposing the purposes and the historical promises of God for his chosen people.

Other views conclude that God will divide the saved into two groups. The first group is a vast multitude of ordinary Christians who will receive an "average" eternal reward. The second group is composed of the spiritual "super-achievers"—martyrs, apostles, great servants of the church, or those who possess some other special merit. Will they have great eternal honors heaped upon them for their outstanding works?

It's important that we try to learn why a group of 144,000 is mentioned in Revelation. The results may determine whether we see God as the loving and impartial Father of all mankind or as an arbitrary and biased Judge. They will also answer this question: Do we accept salvation as the free gift of God, based entirely upon the sacrifice of Christ upon the cross, or is God's grace modified by human genetics or personal righteousness?

Taking It Literally

Revelation 7:1-3 answers the question of Christians under persecution: "How long, O Sovereign Lord?" (6:10). It explains why God did not destroy the wicked world of the first century A.D. and take his people to heaven. The world goes on for the sake of all those who will still be sealed to God (7:3) or redeemed from among men (14:4).

According to Revelation 7:4, the 144,000 is made up entirely from the twelve tribes of Israel. If we take the statement literally, as many do, we immediately run into these difficulties:

1. If only Israelites are going to be marked with a seal, then there will be no Gentiles saved. That's most Christians today. But that idea is in total conflict with Romans 1:16, which says, "I am not ashamed of the gospel, because it is the power of God for the salvation of *everyone* who believes: first for the Jew, then for the *Gentile*." Therefore, we know at the outset that spiritual Israel—the church—is meant and not literal Israel.

2. Ten of the tribes of Israel were taken into Assyrian captivity in 721 B.C. and were absorbed into Gentile nations. So twelve *literal* tribes do not even exist! The twelve tribes are used to represent *spiritual* Israel—all of God's people from every race— everyone present and accounted for.

3. The twelve actual tribes of Israel are not named here. Two tribes, Dan and Ephraim, are omitted; and two, who were not tribes of inheritance, were

inserted—Joseph and Levi. The reason for leaving out Dan and Ephraim is because they were the two idolatrous tribes (1 Kings 12:29; 2 Kings 10:29; Jeremiah 7:15; Hosea 4:17). The Lamb can have no idolaters among his followers.

The reason for including Joseph is obvious. He was actually one of Jacob's twelve sons. He received a double portion of blessing in that of his own two sons, Ephraim and Manasseh, and fathered two tribes of inheritance.

The reason for including Levi is less obvious. As the priestly tribe, they received no tribal division of the land. Instead, Levi had a part in each of the other tribes. Since they were the priestly tribe, they were set apart for service to God. It appears, then, that Levi has been made "common" (in other words, stripped of their priesthood) and that there is no longer a special priesthood. But actually, the reverse is meant. All Christians belong to a holy priesthood (1 Peter 2:9; Revelation 1:6). Every Christian is able to offer praise and sacrifice to God with no mediator but Christ himself.

Focusing Your Faith

1. Based on the concept of the chosen 144,000, do you see God as a loving and impartial Father or as an arbitrary, biased Judge of all mankind? Why?

2. Sing the "new song" you hear the 144,000 singing before the throne.

3. Who does the symbol of 144,000 really stand for?

4. Record some of the reasons why the 144,000 cannot literally be made up entirely of the twelve tribes of Israel.

5. Will there be varying degrees of heavenly rewards—average rewards for ordinary Christians and special rewards for the "high-profile" Christians? What Scripture supports your view?

6. Are you one of the 144,000 described in Revelation? How do you know for certain?

7. Describe how it feels to do battle with Satan's forces knowing that you're a member of the Lord's army.

Chapter Keys

beast   symbolizes a power or institution—political or religious—which is hostile to God and his children.

crown   symbolizes great honor or power.

dragon   represents Satan.

sword   is the symbol of aggressive power, whether good or bad.

white   indicates great age when applied to hair; otherwise it symbolizes purity or sinlessness.

seven   symbolizes salvation or the Savior.

Chapter 5

The Realities of War

The Four Horsemen

⌒⌒

Revelation 6:1-17

Have you ever asked, "Why me, Lord?" If so, you're not alone. Most every living person faces a trauma in his life at some point that causes these questions to be asked: Why do I have cancer . . . or

> ## Key Message:
>
> *Members of the Lord's spiritual army are not exempt from the harsh realities of life.*

epilepsy . . . or AIDS? Why did my mate or my child have to die? Why does God let an unbeliever prosper, while I, a faithful Christian, have financial problems? Why me, Lord? Why is it necessary for me to go through this suffering?

Those are fair questions. The fact is, all these physical problems are the unfortunate realities of the *spiritual war*. Knowing we are physical beings, Satan uses every physical means he can to pull us off guard spiritually. He attacks us physically and causes us to concentrate on things such as starva-

72

Haven't You Heard? There's a WAR Going On! _____

tion, disease, famine, the environment, etc. He
diverts our attention from the even more important
spiritual war.

---

*Have you ever asked, "Why me,
Lord?" If so, you're not alone.*

Satan has so completely deceived mankind that he
has many convinced that God is the one who should
get the blame for the physical consequences of the
war.

Let's look at the realities of this spiritual war as
described in the seals of Revelation.

Opening of the Seals

Revelation 6 is a brief overview of the gospel age.
It is, in effect, a *dramatization* of Matthew 24. The
opening of the six seals do not actually represent a
sequence of historical periods. Rather, they are
significant events that affect the world during the
age of the church. They extend from the time Christ
comes in the person of the indwelling Holy Spirit to
lead his followers, until the end of time, when he
comes to judge the whole earth. They show, from the
viewpoint of human history, what the world will be
like during the gospel age.

The Pharisees' expectation for the messianic age
was that a king of David's house would arise, that he
would sit on David's throne on Mt. Zion. He would be
a warrior-king who would quickly sweep the Romans
into the sea and reign over all nations. There would
be a thousand years of peace and plenty. Every
faithful Jew would sit under his own vine and under
his own fig tree. As one fanciful Pharisee wrote,

"Every vine will have a thousand bunches and every bunch a thousand grapes" (illustrating again the Jewish use of 1,000 to symbolize perfection).

Jesus' disciples were brought up in the traditions of the Pharisees. So, they expected Jesus to restore David's kingdom (Acts 1:6), even though he had taught them that his kingdom was not earthly but spiritual (Luke 17:20, 21). Their lack of spiritual understanding would make them easy marks for false military "messiahs" who would come after Jesus. That's why in Matthew 24:3-14 and in Revelation 6, Jesus makes it clear that he had not come (and would not come) to set up a new world political order of universal peace, plenty, and freedom from disease and disasters.

In Matthew 24:6, 7, Jesus explains that human physical life will go on as it always has. Nations will fight each other, famines will continue to afflict mankind, and earthquakes will keep happening. In fact, his followers will be persecuted, killed, and

_____

Jesus makes it clear that he had not come to set up a new world political order of universal peace, plenty, and freedom from disease and disasters.

_____

hated worldwide for his sake. It will be in this unchanged, hostile world that the gospel must be preached. Only after that will the end come. Revelation 6 repeats the same message, illustrated by dramatic imagery.

The scroll which the Lamb took from the Being on the throne is now about to be opened. It is sealed

74

Haven't You Heard? There's a WAR Going On! _____

with seven seals, suggesting it is the unfolding of the gospel age—the age of salvation. Six of the seals concern the state of the world during the gospel age. The seventh seal concerns the church itself and God's working on its behalf during the gospel age.

The First Seal: Rider on the White Horse

As chapter 6 begins, the Lamb breaks the first of the seven seals, and the drama of the spiritual war begins to unfold. *"I looked, and there before me was a white horse! Its rider held a bow, and he was given a crown, and he rode out as a conqueror bent on conquest"* (vs. 2). Many attempts have been made to identify this dramatic first horseman as a specific historical military figure, such as Alexander the Great or the Roman general, Titus. Such attempts miss the point of the image of the scroll and the seven seals.

The horse is white because it is a spiritual war of purity and righteousness, waged against sin.

This is the gospel age. The crowned conqueror is the same as the rider on the white horse in chapter 19. He's the Lord Jesus Christ who has come to lead the armies of his saints against the forces of evil. He has received all authority on heaven and on earth. He comes in the power and person of the Holy Spirit to begin the gospel age on the first Pentecost after his resurrection from the dead. The horse symbolizes aggressive warfare. This is in contrast with the donkey, an emblem of peace, Christ rode into Jerusalem. The horse is white because it is a spiritual war of purity and righteousness, waged against sin. The arrows stand for the going forth of the gospel message. They are the counterpart of the sword of his mouth in chapter 19.

The emphasis is not, however, upon the rider on the white horse but on the three riders to follow. The parade of riders (like Matthew 24:4-14) is answering these questions: What will the age of the Messiah be like? Does the Prince of Peace come to bring an era of perfect harmony upon the earth? The church at the close of the first century had not experienced the peace and wealth that many had expected. The overthrow of the evil and powerful pagan system had not happened. Jesus had not returned. "What had gone wrong?" the early Christians wondered. And how long would it be before God set things right? "Why, Lord, do we suffer?" they asked. In other words, "Why us, Lord?"

The next three riders answer the question of what the realities of war will be. The text itself explains the symbols of the horsemen.

The Second Seal: Rider on the Red Horse

The second seal is opened: *"Then another horse came out, a fiery red one. Its rider was given power to take peace from the earth and to make men slay each other. To him was given a large sword"* (6:4). This represents physical war, which will continue throughout the Christian age.

Jesus said in Matthew 24:6, 7: "You will hear of wars and rumors of wars, but see to it that you are not alarmed. Such things must happen, but the end is still to come. Nation will rise against nation, and kingdom against kingdom."

There is never a moment in any age when men somewhere are not fighting and killing one another.

Before one war ends, others have already broken out. The gospel age is no different. Times are always going to be tough. But while times are tough in this physical world, Jesus has provided for his army a sense of peace and confidence that defies human logic. He has provided a place of peace in the midst of turmoil. Within his kingdom (the church) "the peace of God which transcends all understanding, will guard [our] hearts and [our] minds in Christ Jesus" (Philippians 4:7).

But in the outside world,
where men do not live by the spirit,
violence and hatred will continue
just as they always have.

This place of peace is the church. There "the wolf and the lamb will feed together, and the lion will eat straw like the ox" (Isaiah 65:25). The powerful and the weak will be brothers and share together. Those who have been cruel and lived by violence will be changed into responsible, productive human beings. Wherever the Spirit dwells in men's hearts there will be "love, joy, peace, patience, kindness, goodness, faithfulness, gentleness and self-control" (Galatians 5:22, 23). But in the outside world, where men do not live by the Spirit, violence and hatred will continue just as they always have. Jesus has given his followers, through his death on the cross, the power to have peace in the midst of pain, just as he had inner peace during the flesh-ripping pain of that cross. The knowledge that we are spiritually safe within the fortress of his love allows us that soul-soothing peace and calm that outsiders cannot know.

The Third Seal: Rider on the Black Horse

The third seal is opened, and *"there before me was a black horse! Its rider was holding a pair of scales in his hand,"* (6:5b) and a voice proclaims: *"A quart of wheat for a day's wages, and three quarts of barley for a day's wages, and do not damage the oil and the wine"* (6:6b). A quart of grain was the daily ration for an adult (and still is in much of the world). It is not a complete or wholesome diet, but it will sustain life. A man could eat wheat bread for his daily wages, or, if he was willing to accept the coarser barley bread, he would have enough for a small family.

We can picture the setting: a small village store has open sacks of grain standing against the counter. The sour-faced merchant speaks to a shabby laborer who has just shuffled in: "All right, you! Get your grain and leave before you knock over

The black horse represents physical famine or hunger.

the containers of oil and wine, which you could never pay for!" Good food is sold in the shop, but it's only for the well-to-do people. The peasants can only dream of eating it.

The world's teeming millions will live all their lives from hand to mouth in the messianic (gospel) age, just as they have always done. But the most important symbol is the scales. The black horse represents physical famine or hunger. The scales imply that there is still something available to be measured, but its distribution will be determined by commercial interests. Some people who are wealthy will have more than they need, but the majority will not have enough. There is normally enough food on earth to feed its population reasonably well, but it will never be distributed on the basis of need. The fact is, on an average day, 70 percent of the world's population goes to bed hungry. Some people will be able to feed their dogs and cats red meat, while in other places millions of people don't taste meat themselves from one month to the next. It has

---

The fact is, on an average day, 70 percent of the world's population goes to bed hungry.

---

always been so, and it will always be so. The rider on the black horse shows that although in the gospel age those who hunger and thirst for righteousness will be filled (Matthew 5:6), famine will always take its terrible toll on the earth's people (Matthew 24:7).

The Fourth Seal: Rider on the Pale Horse

The Lamb breaks the fourth seal, and *"there before me was a pale horse! Its rider was named Death, and Hades was following close behind him"* (6:8b). The color of the horse is literally "pale green" (Greek, *chloros*). It's the color of grass that has been kept covered for a period of time. It suggests the greenish pallor of people physically sick with a deadly fever. It is identified as "plague" in Revelation 6:8—such as the raging epidemics which have destroyed a large part of the earth's population from time to time. Three such physical plagues have been so terminal that they were actually named "death": smallpox (the red death), bubonic plague (the black death), and tuberculosis (the white death). Malaria and cholera may have killed even more than those three. And it now appears that AIDS may prove to be the most deadly physical plague of all.

> *The color of the horse is literally "pale green." It suggests the greenish pallor of people physically sick with a deadly fever.*

John makes the Greek distinction between d*eath* (the point at which life stops) and *Hades* (Greek, "not seen"—the place of the dead). The Hebrews used the term *Sheol* for the state of the dead. Sometimes Sheol means no more than the grave, but sometimes it means a place where the wicked go after death. Hades didn't always imply a place of punishment. Rather, it was the common state of the dead, whether they were wicked or righteous. As war, famine and disease, earthquakes, and wild beasts bring death, so Hades carries them away to an unseen state.

The Fifth Seal: The Souls Under the Altar

As the fifth seal is opened, *"I saw under the altar the souls of those who had been slain because of the word of God and the testimony they had maintained"* (6:9). The scene has changed from what is happening in the world to what is happening to Christ's people. Jesus had warned: "Then you will be handed over to be persecuted and put to death, and you will be hated by all nations because of me . . . but he who stands firm to the end will be saved" (Matthew 24:9, 13).

Even as John writes Revelation, the church is under savage persecution in various places. The Christians are actually wondering what has happened to God. Why does he allow them to suffer—even to be killed? "Why us, Lord?" All faithful Christians are, in a sense, martyrs. We "die" to the physical world by giving up its evil pleasures to live for Christ. Yet we continue to suffer the same physical calamities as sinners who won't repent.

John sees the souls of the martyrs under the altar and hears them cry out, *"How long, Sovereign Lord, holy and true, until you judge the inhabitants of the earth and avenge our blood?"* (6:10). They simply can't believe that the Lord will allow the evil to go on. They have an intense longing for the coming of Jesus and the end of the world. They were expressing a longing for justice—an innate desire of every right-thinking human.

Not one drop of blood (or sweat) shed in the service of Christ is ever unnoticed by God. It is a constant testimony to him until everything is made right. The symbol of the altar is used because the brazen altar was where sacrifices were made to God. Literally, the altar is the earth where the martyrs were killed. They are under the altar because they are buried in the earth. But God never forgets where they are. Until they are avenged, the wrongs done to them forever ring in his ears. God said, "It is mine to avenge; I will repay. Their day of disaster is near and their doom rushes upon them" (Deuteronomy 32:35).

Each one of the saints is given a white robe (the perfect righteousness of Jesus Christ and their assurance of eternal salvation.) They are told they must wait until God's purpose for the world is realized. There are still other saints coming to God. He is saying to the martyrs, "Wait for your brothers and sisters in Christ who are still to come; we cannot close the door on those still on the way." God, as Peter says, "is not willing that any should perish!" (2 Peter 3:9).

The Sixth Seal: The Final Scene

The sixth seal is the last seal in the sequence because the seventh seal is a separate series of events which outlines dramatic events of history from the standpoint of the church.

At the opening of the sixth seal *"there was a great earthquake. The sun turned black . . . , the whole moon turned blood red, and the stars in the sky fell to earth. . . . The sky receded like a scroll, . . . and every mountain and island was removed from its place"* (6:12-14). This description follows the pattern of the prophetic formula for judgment. We find this formula a number of times in the Old Testament. Although they have varying details, each one describes a dramatic intervention of God in earthly affairs. Generally, it does not refer to the final judgment, but to the passing of an era of time or a worldly system.[1] It's not important how literally

[1]In Isaiah 13 it predicts the destruction of Babylon; in Isaiah 34 it tells of the coming destruction of Edom; Ezekiel 31 announces Egypt's destruction; and Joel 2 and 3 foretell the destruction of Jerusalem. Jesus applies the formula to the destruction of the Jewish system (by the Romans in A.D. 70) in Matthew 24:29, quoting from Isaiah 13:10 and 34:4. But Revelation 6 appears to be talking about the final destruction of the physical universe and the great day of the last judgment. Read Luke 21:25-28 for a comparison.

such images are interpreted. The purpose of the vivid language is to give assurance to the Christians who are wondering if the unjust world system will ever end. The answer is this: your enemies may appear powerful now, but they and all ungodly men will one day cower in hiding places as the solar system comes apart before their eyes. The day of God's wrath is surely coming—the day in which they will be destroyed forever. Peter used similar language to give assurance to Christians under persecution: "You ought to live holy and godly lives as you look forward to the day of God and speed its coming. That day will bring about the destruction of the heavens by fire, and the elements will melt in the heat" (2 Peter 3:11, 12).

The truth is, Christians don't come up out of the spiritual watery grave of baptism into a perfect world of physical peace and wealth.

The truth is, Christians don't come up out of the spiritual watery grave of baptism into a perfect world of physical peace and wealth. As physical beings, we must face all the daily trauma, threatening world events, diseases, and death that the rest of mankind must face—both believers and unbelievers. We are not physically exempt from normal life. These are the realities of the spiritual war.

Here's the difference for us: We are spiritually exempt. This physical life is only temporary. After its finish, we will soar into the presence of our gracious God to live in peace and in heavenly wealth forever. But wait! Spiritual peace and wealth are not "out there somewhere." Through the cross, Christ has given us the power to have spiritual peace in the midst of physical pain and trials—just as he had on the cross—until the Day of the Lord shall come.

And, oh, what a day that will be! For the unrepentant sinner it will be a time of terror beyond the description of human language; for the saved it's the glorious dawning of paradise regained!

Come, Lord Jesus!

Focusing Your Faith

1. Have you ever asked, "Why me, Lord?" Describe that time in your life.

2. What does the second horse in Revelation 6:4 represent? What's the clue?

3. How do you feel about the statement in James 1:2, "Consider it pure joy my brothers whenever you face trials of many kinds . . . "?

4. Compare 2 Peter 3:11, 12 with God's message in Revelation 6. Are the messages different or alike?

5. Imagine you are teaching a group of plague-ridden, third-world Christians. What would your message be?

6. How do you see the current AIDS epidemic in relation to Revelation 6:8? What is our responsibility as Christians?

7. Is it more important to respond to the desperate cries of suffering Christians or non-Christians?

Chapter Keys

golden   *denotes something very precious or luxurious.*

lamps   *stand for truth.*

star   *symbolizes heralds or messengers.*

white   *indicates great age when applied to hair; otherwise it symbolizes purity or sinlessness.*

7   *symbolizes salvation or the Savior.*

10   *represents abstract completeness (a perfection of quality, rather than numerical completeness). Ten expresses the ultimate degree of anything, whether extremely good and holy or extremely bad and wicked.*

Chapter 6

Satan's First
Battlefront

The Seven Churches

∞

Revelation 2:1–3:1-22

Key Message:

A life-changing church is the greatest threat to Satan's ultimate victory. He is relentless in his efforts to destroy it.

Nowhere is the battle between Christ and Satan more fierce than in the church of God itself. In some congregations Satan masquerades as an angel of light. He has a foothold stronger in some than in others, but nowhere is he inactive. He has not given up his most cherished goal—to destroy the church, the sanctuary of the saved.

The church is where Satan wages his first battlefront; it's his primary battleground. Only through the church and its message of Christ's saving blood can Satan be defeated . . . and he knows it. If he loses the battle in the church, he loses the war. So, from a strategic standpoint, Satan's insidious and most vicious attacks will be launched against the church. His agents infiltrate the church and look for weak places in the fortress walls to attack. Do not be deceived into believing that Satan doesn't come to church.

John sees the battle between good and evil vividly portrayed in each of the seven churches of Asia, which represent various aspects of Christ's universal church. What Christ says to these seven churches in Revelation, he is saying to the church as a whole today: "Some things you're doing are good, some are bad."

> ### *Satan and his entire army of angels are as active today as in any time in history as they pursue their ultimate goal—the destruction of the church.*

Satan and his entire army of angels are as active today as in any time in history as they pursue their ultimate goal—the destruction of the church. His ugly face shows itself repeatedly in the church. Can we see him? Do we recognize the many faces of the enemy in God's church today?

The letters to the seven churches of Asia comprise a distinct section of the Book of Revelation. It is introduced with dramatic fanfare. The Alpha and the Omega, resplendent beyond measure, stands in the middle of the seven golden lampstands and speaks to John in a voice as awe-inspiring as a mighty waterfall. He holds seven stars in his right hand, and his face is as brilliant as the sun. After instructing John to write what he has seen, and the things that are occurring and will occur, he explains the lampstands and the stars.

The seven lampstands represent the seven churches, and the seven stars represent their messengers (the Greek term *angelos* means "messenger"). In this context, evangelists are likely meant.

Some scholars believe that the best interpretation of this passage is a literal one, and that John refers to the seven actual churches named in Revelation. Others hold that the seven churches represent seven different ages of church history. Still others believe that the messages to the seven churches are simply a format for addressing problems and challenges that are common to churches in any age. We will assume the last position as the best explanation for the Holy Spirit's purpose in including the reference.

Tradition says the apostle John spent most of his later years working among the churches of Asia Minor, scattered throughout the region around Ephesus. But that would not explain the number seven, since there were other known congregations in Asia Minor that are not named. Probably the number seven is to be taken in its symbolic sense as the *salvation number* and means only that these letters are to the saved—to Christians wherever and whenever they live. Some points of identification in

> *... the messages to the seven churches are simply a format for addressing problems and challenges that are common to churches in any age.*

the letters do pertain to the individual congregations, making it quite possible, even probable, that these churches were specifically chosen because they represent strengths and weaknesses of the universal church. They serve as a mirror in which we can examine and evaluate our own quality of fellowship and commitment.

The letters contain commendations for strengths, rebukes for shortcomings, and promises for the Lord's faithful and victorious servants. They exhibit the great tug-of-war that goes on between Christ and Satan for the heart of every church. They show the skirmishes and battles being won by each side.

Ephesus

Good: Hard work and perseverance.

Christians do not earn their salvation by doing good works. We are saved by God's sweet grace through our faith in him. But we are created in Christ Jesus to do good works (Ephesians 2:8, 10). A bird does not become a bird because he sings; he sings because he is already a bird. In the same way,

---

[The letters to the seven churches]
exhibit the great
tug-of-war that goes on between
Christ and Satan for the heart of
every church.

---

a Christian does not become saved because he does good works; he does good works because he *is already saved*. A saving faith always expresses itself in service. If good deeds are not present, saving faith is not present (James 2:14-26). Perseverance is the proof of a genuine new birth. Shallow faith is like

the rocky soil of Jesus' parable (Matthew 13:5, 6); it
will not support growth for very long, even though it
may show great promise at first. If we give up, it is
just as if we had never left the world of sin (Ezekiel
18:24). The Christians at Ephesus continued doing
good works, which was evidence of their true experience of the new birth. They understood they had
been made "new creatures" in order to do good
works.

Evil: "You have forsaken your first love."

The Ephesian Christians had not given up working for the Lord, but their motivation or reason for
doing their work had changed. They no longer
worked out of a sense of gratitude in response to the
grace and love of God. Legalism, or the earning of
salvation by works, obviously was their primary
problem. The Holy Spirit was not displeased with
what they were doing, but *why* they were doing it. If
Satan can convince Christians they can work enough
to be saved, he has accomplished his primary goal.
Like the Corinthian church and some Hebrew Christians, they had not developed in love as they should
have (1 Corinthians 3:1-3; Hebrews 5:12) but had, in
fact, slipped backward. God never accepts the status
quo as a goal for the future. The Ephesians were in
danger of having their lampstand taken away (being
rejected by the Lord as his true church).

Smyrna

Good: Spiritual wealth in spite of physical poverty and affliction.

Many Christians, even most of those of the first
century, were economically poor. In spite of their
physical circumstances, they were able to rejoice

even when they lost everything for their faith (Hebrews 10:34). The Christians in Smyrna had learned the secret of true contentment (1 Timothy 6:6-8), even though some of them faced death. That contentment was a great spiritual treasure.

Evil: The Lord could find nothing to condemn in the church of Smyrna.

What a tribute! They were overcoming Satan by doing the best they could, even though they were slandered and impoverished. These noble Christians are precious examples to follow.

Pergamum

Good: Remaining True to Christ's Name.

The name "Christian" honors God's children above measure. The God of the universe allows us to wear his very own name. Yet the name has come to mean little more in our world than differentiating its wearer from the Muslims and Buddhists. When professed followers of the Lord Jesus follow a lifestyle that blends easily with the conduct of the average people of the world, then they have not remained true to Christ's name. The Israelites boasted that they were children of the true God and yet lived no better than the pagans around them. In so doing, they dishonored God's name (Ezekiel 36:19-21). In contrast, the Christians of Pergamum did not wear the name of Christ casually and so dishonor it. Indeed, to wear it at all put their lives in deadly peril! Still, they openly proclaimed the Lordship of Jesus, even after one of their leaders was martyred for the faith. Christians today must wear the name openly, humbly, and fearlessly.

Evil: "I have a few things against you."

Even though Satan was the controlling power over their community, the Christians of Pergamum had not given in to him, even when faithful Antipas was killed. Still there were some things being tolerated in the church that were abominable to God!

The teaching of Balaam: During the wilderness wanderings of Israel, the corrupt prophet Balaam advised Balak that the way to destroy the Israelites was to seduce them, to cause them to compromise their faith. So the Midianites sacrificed animals to their gods and persuaded the children of Israel to eat the meat and join them in the immoral rites that accompanied their worship. Christians of the New Testament period were sometimes tempted to participate in the pagan sacrifices and temple rites of the day in order to escape persecution. The so-called "Balaamites" were those who taught that it was all right to participate in the heathen ceremonies as long as you did not really believe in them. Such spiritual compromise was one of the most serious problems in the Corinthian church (1 Corinthians 8; 2 Corinthians 6:14-18).

The Nicolaitans. According to tradition, the doctrine of the Nicolaitans stemmed from Nicolas, a convert to Judaism from Antioch, who was chosen to be one of the seven deacons to serve the Jerusalem church (Acts 6:5). The Nicolaitans held liberal views about the Christian lifestyle. They argued that it would be more effective not to follow a distinctive code of behavior that might lead to unpopularity in the Roman world. This was their answer to the problem of how to be different without appearing "odd."

But unless Christians have a standard of morals and ethics above the general level of behavior, we have nothing better to offer the world than what it already has. We struggle because we do not want to be seen by the world as impractical fanatics. It was obviously of great importance to Jesus that the brethren at Pergamum live in such a way that they were witnesses to the life-changing influence of the gospel and that they challenge and oppose those who taught differently. In our society today, the devil tempts the church to tolerate things that are abominations to God. He teaches us to worship at the

---

No doubt, Jesus feels the same urgency today as he always has for his followers to be witnesses to the life-changing influence of the gospel.

---

shrines of competitive sport, materialism, popularity, and power. He leads us to participate in pagan and immoral rites, such as witchcraft, while denying at the same time that we follow Satan. He "helps" us water down our stand against behavior that destroys the family, such as unmarried people living together, in the name of "accepting people where they are" and "being nonjudgmental."

No doubt, Jesus feels the same urgency today as he always has for his followers to be witnesses to the life-changing influence of the gospel.

Thyatira

Good: Love, faith, service, perseverance, and increasing commitment.

According to John, the Thyatiran Christians were

more deeply dedicated to serving the Lord than when they first became Christians. They were serving with more heart and with greater tenacity than they ever had because of their growing love and faith. Only true love for God and man and an abiding trust in the Lord lets us experience the spiritual growth that God expects of his children.

Evil: "You tolerate that woman."

There was a self-styled prophetess in the church at Thyatira who claimed to teach the "deep things" of the Christian faith. Her name probably was not Jezebel, but John's use of the name was likely a symbolic allusion to Ahab's wife (1 Kings 16:30-33) who brought Baal-worship to Israel. The wicked woman of Thyatira was corrupting the church by encouraging fellowship with idolaters. So the problem there appears to be very much the same as the one at Pergamum. But in every age, the dilemma exists for the Christian: how to be effective _in_ the world without being part _of_ the world.

Sardis

Good: "You have a few people in Sardis who have not soiled their clothes."

It is reassuring to earnest Christians to know that we are not saved or lost by congregation-sized units. The Lord does not give an average grade to the total membership of a church and condemn or reward it accordingly. Each of us will be personally accountable to God (Romans 14:12). Even in a congregation that is a disgrace to the Lord's name, as Sardis was, there will be some who "walk with Jesus, dressed in white."

Evil: "You are dead. . . . I have not found your deeds complete."

This was a "housekeeping" church. The original Greek actually says, "You have a name that you live, but you are dead." They held onto the name of Christ but did nothing to show they had a right to it. Nothing planned ever happened; nothing was accomplished. Like yeast in dough, the influence of the church is supposed to have an impact on the world around it. Like the Judah of Jeremiah's day, the Sardians were "playing church"—observing the proper forms and assemblies, but living unchanged lives. If we hang our religion on the front door of the church, we are self-centered and hypocritical obstacles to the glory of God. Men will praise God when they see his children letting their lights shine through good works.

Philadelphia

Good: "You have little strength, yet you have kept my word and have not denied my name."

Their enemies, "the synagogue of Satan," had apparently done them serious damage and made their struggle difficult. Adverse circumstances, though, had not provoked them to renounce the faith or deny that they were Christians. It is during just such troubling times when Christians must rely upon the Lord's strength to survive, that great individual spiritual growth results—even though uncontrollable circumstances slow or stop numerical growth. The Philadelphians had patiently endured great hardship. What a great lesson for us in the church today! In these times of social warfare with the devil, the church must deflect his arrows— economic pressure, false church leadership, family failures, racial prejudice, legalism, traditionalism, and cheap grace, to name a few. Like the Philadelphians, we must patiently endure his attacks, knowing the war has already been won.

Evil: One of two churches (with Smyrna) with whom the Lord found no fault.

Like Smyrna, they were being placed in jeopardy (presumably with the Roman government) by slanderous lies from the Jewish community who had by this time become bitter enemies of the Christians. The earlier cordial relations with Jews (apart from the temple hierarchy) as reflected in the early part of Acts (2:27; 4:1-21) had by this time changed into hostility. A possible explanation is that many Jewish synagogues had lost significant numbers of members to the Christian community. Because the Philadelphian brethren had not given in to persecution, the Lord would give them an open door. This possibly indicates that he would see that their saving message and influence would not be hindered.

God will also open doors of opportunity today to his people who don't give in to persecution. Their influence will be widely felt, and their message will not be hindered. The "open-door" policy of God is still intact!

Laodicea

Good: The Lord could find nothing at all to commend in the Laodicean church.

They did nothing to change the world or themselves because the devil had gained complete control.

Evil: "Because you are lukewarm . . . I am about to spit you out of my mouth."

The Laodicean Christians were economically and socially prosperous. It is significant that in a time of general persecution of Christians in the Roman world, they had no problems. That suggests that they did not impress their pagan friends as being too much different from themselves.

Human beings tend to evaluate according to scales of measurement or percentage. To us, on a scale of one to ten, five is much better than zero. Not so in the Lord's system of evaluation; five is much worse than zero. Why? Because it's mediocre. Less damage is done to the work of God's kingdom by a blasphemous atheist than by a lukewarm Christian, because the atheist is not regarded by the world as a representative of religion, and the lukewarm Christian is.

The typical inhabitant of any country is not a Bible reader, so he will never learn about Christianity from its pages. He judges the Christian religion by what he sees in his professed Christian friend or neighbor. Too often, what he sees there gives him no motivation to become a Christian himself.

The Lord ends each of the seven letters with this admonition: "He who has an ear, let him hear what the Spirit says to the churches" (3:22). We can see ourselves mirrored in many of the shortcomings of the churches of Asia. The tug-of-war continues in every congregation of the church today. Satan and his forces of evil are on one side of the rope; Christ and his forces of good are on the other. Those churches ceased to exist long ago, but their examples—good and bad—serve as a standard of self-measurement for those of us for whom it is not yet too late. For further study on the promises to the seven churches in Revelation 2–3, see Appendix 4.

Focusing Your Faith

1. What is Satan's ultimate goal on the earth?

2. Identify at least three specific areas in the life of your church where Satan has a foothold. What power has God provided in each area to shake him loose?

3. Imagine that you could see Satan as a lion stalking your every step, wanting to devour you. How do you feel?

4. When have you seen Satan masquerading as an angel of light? Read 2 Corinthians 11:14.

5. If the apostle who wrote to the seven churches of Asia also wrote to your congregation, what commendations would you hear him giving?

6. How do you think the Ephesian church in Revelation 2:4 demonstrated that they had forsaken their first love? Could the apostle write this message to your congregation?

7. List the characteristics of a lukewarm church, such as the one in Laodicea.

Chapter Keys

beast usually symbolizes a power or institution—political or religious—which is hostile to God and his children.

gold denotes something very precious or luxurious.

horns most often represent powers or kings.

lamb is the symbol for Christ—the sacrificial offering for sin.

one hour
  symbolizes an indefinite time period.

purple was an extremely expensive dye, and clothing of that color was only worn by royalty or the very rich.

scarlet was not as expensive as purple but still very costly. The two colors were paired as tokens of royalty.

waters is used for pagan nations, sources of truth; its roaring signifies an authoritative voice.

7 symbolizes salvation or the Savior.

10 represents abstract completeness (a perfection of quality, rather than numerical completeness). Ten expresses the ultimate degree of anything, whether extremely good and holy or extremely bad and wicked.

Chapter 7

Satan's Second
Battlefront

The Great Prostitute

∽

Key Message:

Satan, in the form of civil government, infiltrates the true church and brings about the great apostasy.

Satan is a master battle strategist. He has already mounted attacks of external persecution against the church. He has even created destructive mischief within and among the body itself. But dissatisfied that he cannot destroy the true church, he has devised a second strategic front—the apostate church.

The two beasts of Revelation 13 vividly illustrate how Satan used the governing authorities of the world to further his destructive mission of persecution. An overview of this chapter will give us a better grasp of the full implication of the great apostasy of the church which is addressed in chapter 17. For further information, see Appendix 5, The Two Beasts, in the back of this book.

Chapter 13 details the first beast as a wild, man-eating predator who is clothed in a composite costume of a leopard, a bear, and a lion and has seven heads. From Babylon to Rome, the four great pagan empires that succeeded one another preyed upon God's chosen people—first the Israelites and then the followers of Christ. The part of the beast that relates to the overall persecution of the church itself is the seven heads, which represent the seven stages of Roman power. The head that specifically pertains to the persecution is the sixth head—imperial Rome. The Roman emperors led Satan's attack against the

---

[The second beast] is a lamb with two horns, which represents the marriage of secular and religious power.

---

church for 250 years. Fortunately, they did not succeed, except on the fringes, in harming the growth of Christianity. Although they killed untold thousands of Christians and caused terrible suffering, their attempts to wipe out the faith actually pruned away the weak branches and left the church stronger than it had been when the persecution started. Satan's continued attacks on the local churches simply failed overall.

Then a remarkable thing happened. The old pagan empire of Rome suddenly disintegrated, and a new political day dawned. It was much like the collapse of communism in our time. A brilliant, handsome young general seized the Roman throne, and the long night of persecution for the church was seemingly over. The first "Christian" Roman emperor,

Constantine the Great, ruled over the world. He
promised to make Christianity the new state religion, and church leaders from all over the Mediterranean world flocked to pay him homage.

There was rejoicing and praise, because the old
ugly head of pagan Rome had received the death-
stroke. The first beast was dead. But wait—Satan,
the great strategist, had worked an ingenious illusion. The wounded head was healed, and the beast
lived again as the second beast, but how different
this one looks!

The second beast is nothing like the fire-breath-
ing, raging first beast. He is a lamb with two horns,
which represents the marriage of secular and religious power. Like Jacob's disguise to defraud Esau
of the blessing of Isaac, Satan has now disguised his
beast in the skin-and-horns costume of a lamb—the
symbol of Christ. But, he was not successful in
disguising the voice, for when the lamb spoke it was
the voice of Satan himself. However, for many,
seeing is believing, and most of the world succumbed
to the clever deception. Once again, all roads led to
Rome—a rejuvenated Rome that was more brilliant
and powerful than ever before—the second beast.

Falling Away from Christ

Like John, Paul was led by the Holy Spirit, and
he wanted to make certain that the Thessalonians
understood that a great "falling away from Christ,"
or apostasy, would happen before Christ's return.
He advised them that they not "become easily un-
settled or alarmed by some prophecy," and that they
might not let themselves be deceived by anyone
(2 Thessalonians 2:2, 3). John outlines the great fall
in Revelation 13 and 17 so that the people may
recognize and avoid it. Otherwise, they might take

part in its sins and share in its judgment (Revelation 18:4, 5).

It would be naive to think that Satan has stopped promoting apostasy. His whole purpose is to destroy the church of God. He did not succeed in stopping Christianity by persecution, so, he infiltrated the church itself and became "one of us." In that way he succeeded in diverting and perverting a major part of the Christian movement. The church's most dangerous enemies come from within. Just as the Holy Spirit said through Paul: "Even from your own number men will arise and distort the truth in order to draw away disciples after them. So be on your guard!" (Acts 20:30, 31).

It would be naive to think that Satan has stopped promoting apostasy. His whole purpose is to destroy the church of God.

This Satan-based distortion of truth, Paul tells us, will reveal the "man of lawlessness," who will "oppose and exalt himself over everything that is called God or is worshiped," and even "sets himself up in God's temple, proclaiming himself to be God" (2 Thessalonians 2:3, 4).

The symbol of the great prostitute in Revelation 17 shows how Satan, disguised as a supporter of Christianity in the costume of the Holy Roman Empire, tempts the army of God to follow a new lover. They fall away from God, their true love, and make love to Satan himself—the prostitute, the church of Rome.

The Great Prostitute

"One of the seven angels who had the seven bowls came and said to me, 'Come, I will show you the punishment of the great prostitute, who sits on many waters. With her the kings of the earth committed adultery and the inhabitants of the earth were intoxicated with the wine of her adulteries.'

"Then the angel carried me away in the Spirit into a desert. There I saw a woman sitting on a scarlet beast that was covered with blasphemous names and had seven heads and ten horns. The woman was dressed in purple and scarlet, and was glittering with gold, precious stones and pearls. She held a golden cup in her hand, filled with abominable things and the filth of her adulteries. This title was written on her forehead: MYSTERY, BABYLON THE GREAT, THE MOTHER OF PROSTITUTES AND OF THE ABOMINATIONS OF THE EARTH. I saw that the woman was drunk with the blood of the saints, the blood of those who bore testimony to Jesus.

"When I saw her, I was greatly astonished" (Revelation 17:1-6).

Chapter 17 is really an expansion of chapter 13. It focuses on the development of religious Rome—the seventh head of the beast. There is still the beast with seven heads and ten horns, but now there is a woman riding on the beast. And the beast himself has changed from the weird costume of the leopard, bear, and lion to "a scarlet beast." This identifies the creature more closely with the red dragon—Satan (12:3, 9). Red is also the color of violence and warfare (6:3, 4).

The woman, called "the great prostitute" (vs.1), is richly dressed in royal robes of purple and scarlet and wearing gold and jewels. She is also shown sitting on "many waters," which are the multitudes of different peoples and nations (vs. 15). She holds a golden cup in her hand—the symbol of her evil practices. The writing on her forehead (frontlet) suggests a connection with the frontlet of the Jewish high priest, which said "Holiness to Yahweh." Apparently, this prostitute claims to be the mediator between God and man, since that is the function of a high priest. But instead of mediating God's grace, she administers things that are hated by God. She is a prostitute because she both commits spiritual adultery against God and seduces even kings to do the same. Spiritual adultery is idolatry.

She is a prostitute because she both commits spiritual adultery against God and seduces even kings to do the same.

The ideas inherent in the "wine" of her adulteries and the golden cup have suggested the chalice of the Roman Catholic Mass to many interpreters. There are many who find it judgmental and offensive to apply chapters 13 and 17 to the Roman church, because there are many deeply dedicated and benevolent people who are affiliated with the Latin church. Revelation 18:4 recognizes that fact. Nevertheless, there are several points of identification between those chapters and the Roman Catholic Church (particularly the church of the Middle Ages) which are difficult to otherwise explain. Some of these similarities are detailed at the end of this chapter.

Her Idolatry and Power

"Babylon the Great" is attached to the prostitute. It refers to the ancient Mesopotamian city that was the center of idolatrous worship of the sun god, Marduk, and was the site of the great towering ziggurat in that god's honor (possibly the tower that "reaches up to the heavens," Genesis 11:4). This city described in Revelation 17 is "the great Babylon." In other words, it's a greater city than ancient Babylon ever was but equally a center of idolatry. Again, this obviously refers to Rome.

In addition to representing the seven hills upon which the woman sits, the seven heads of the beast stand for seven kings. At the writing of Revelation, five of them have passed, one is in existence, and one is still future. But the beast also has ten horns (the symbol for power), representing ten kings who are to reign in the future "for one hour" (at the same time), whose authority is "along with the beast." In other words, their ten kingdoms are sub-states of the beast whom they will serve for a limited time. During this period the ten kings will make war against the Lamb (probably referring to the Inquisition, a former Roman Catholic tribunal of severe questioning for the purpose of discovering and punishing heresy).

The Holy Roman Empire began when the pope crowned Charlemagne (king of the Franks) as Holy Roman Emperor on Christmas Day, A.D. 800. The names and geographical boundaries of the countries involved changed through the centuries, but ten was the typical number of kingdoms that made up the Holy Roman Empire. These kingdoms served the interests of Rome for a time. Without realizing it, the pope had created a monster, but for a time it kept him at the top of secular and religious power. The Inquisition itself was not directly carried out by

108

Haven't You Heard? There's a WAR Going On! _____

the church. The victims were pronounced heretics by the church (generally by members of the Dominican order), but the condemned persons were turned over to the secular authorities for execution. Often they were burned at the stake.

Satan is out in full force with his army of evil, dressed as angels of light, infiltrating the church both locally and universally with heresies and distortions of the truth.

Although the ten kingdoms consolidated the pope's power over Europe, in the end they rebelled and virtually destroyed the papacy. First, the German emperor, Henry IV, turned on the Vatican. A war of attrition followed that left both Germany and Rome weakened. Henry VIII of England cut ties between his country and the Catholic church. But the most devastating blow was dealt by the king of France, Philip the Fair, who, after a series of confrontations with Rome, sent an army to arrest and imprison the pope and then moved the Vatican to Avignon in France, where he could control it.

Almost a century followed when there were three popes, with various countries acknowledging one of them as the head of the church. Rome was almost reduced to a ghost town because the tourist trade dried up. It was openly predicted by some scholars that the Roman Catholic Church would not survive the disaster, but of course it did and has more members and wealth today than it has ever had in history. And, to be fair, it probably operates more orphanages, hospitals, and schools than all Protestant denominations put together. It has many brilliant scholars and countless self-sacrificing missionaries, who set an example of dedicated service to that which they believe. (More information about this subject is included at the end of this chapter.)

Satan's Purpose Is Unchanged

Apostasy, or falling away from Christ, doesn't occur exclusively at the highest levels of governments and "religious" institutions. Satan carries out his strategy of apostasy at the local level as well today.

Satan's purpose has not changed. He is out in full force with his army of evil, dressed as angels of light, infiltrating the church both locally and universally with heresies and distortions of the truth. His weapons are deceit, tolerance of false teachings, patience with popular sins, and—perhaps most telling of all—apathy. He is devious and dirty; he doesn't fight fairly. He hits us in our weakest spots and tempts us to leave the true Lamb of God. He's a liar and a con man who will stop at nothing to destroy the church— one Christian at a time, one congregation at a time. And he's even prepared to approach us as our best Christian friend.

But despite his meek and harmless appearance, he cannot disguise his evil voice. Praise be to God for his eternal Word, the true voice of the Lamb.

The following information has been included in this chapter for supplemental study.

_____

Applying Revelation 13 and 17 to the Roman Catholic Church

1. Rome, is without question, the great city referred to as ruling over the earth when John wrote (11:8). It was a city built on seven hills (17:9). It was the fourth phase of the great world kingdom beginning with Babylon (comparing Daniel 7, 8 with Revelation 13).

2. The second beast is built upon the ruins of the Roman Empire (the kingdom which received the fatal wound but was restored, 13:3).

3. The second beast looks like Christ the Lamb but deceives people into paying homage to Rome. It is, therefore, a religious institution based upon the Roman Empire (13:11, 12).

4. This false church set up a man as the symbol of the church and persecuted to death those who would not worship him (13:15).

5. Rome fought the true church and prevailed, except for those whose names are written in the book of life (13:8).

6. The Catholic church is a super-kingdom which controls kings and forces them to obey its commands (17:13).

7. It is a fabulously wealthy organization (17:4).

Focusing Your Faith

1. From where do the church's most dangerous enemies come?

2. What are the historical clues that help you identify the Great Prostitute as the Holy Roman Empire? Make a list.

3. In what sense can we say that Satan has used our government to diminish the effectiveness of the church?

4. What is your emotional response to the fact that Satan intends to have his agents infiltrate your church?

5. Describe the most obvious false religion in your community.

6. Identify a religion dominated by government control today.

7. List several ways in which the media promotes godless, false religion in movies, television and print.

Chapter Keys

crown   *symbolizes great honor or power. In Revelation 9:7 it represents the bronze helmets worn by the Goths.*

five months
    would be a span of 150 years divided into five periods, because the Hebrews used "days" as symbolic of years.

gold   *denotes something very precious or luxurious.*

key   *represents authority. The person with the key had power over the house or kingdom to open or close the door.*

mountain
    symbolizes a community of strength—a kingdom.

sea   *symbolizes the pagan world.*

star   *symbolizes heralds or messengers.*

Chapter 8

God's
Counterattack

God's Use of World Powers

✧

Revelation 9:1-11

Key Message:

God accomplishes his purpose for the kingdom by controlling world events.

As finite humans, we have difficulty seeing the infinite plan and overview battle strategy of our Commander-in-Chief—God. Our vision is so limited by our own time and our own space that we tend to interpret God's Word, especially Revelation, from our own vantage point in the battle. This is in contrast to God's limitless vision which is like the general who has the advantage of global surveillance for his view of the *entire war*! God sees clearly every moment of time from creation to judgment.

We must be careful not to get so caught up in applying exact historical events to Revelation that we lose sight of the main point—God is using *all* of history to work out his victorious war strategies, not just the short time we have here on earth. This point is amazingly clear when we consider how accurately God revealed to John the future events described in Revelation. They were future events to John, but they are history to us. God saw them all in accurate detail with his divine vision.

God is using all of history to work out his victorious war strategies.

Revelation 9 shows that God never abandons his people to the mindless progression of human affairs. He didn't just wind up the world like a toy top and set it down on the floor of the universe to spin itself out. He can and does intervene to work out his ultimate goal—the salvation of as many people as possible through his Son, Jesus Christ.

It appeared to many Christians who were being persecuted in John's time that God had deserted them and left the devil in charge of the world. Chapter 9 makes it clear that God knows what will happen, even in the far-distant future. He also has the most significant role in determining how history unfolds. He is a hands-on God, not some aloof top spinner. He already planned a counterattack to defeat Satan's ambush against the church through the Roman Empire.

The Counterattack

In Revelation 7, we were introduced to the saved—the symbolic army of 144,000. Since chapter 8 begins with the opening of the seventh seal, we can expect a connection with salvation or the saved.

The scene is in heaven, where an angel with a

golden censer for burning incense offers the prayers of the saints to God. The answer comes as fire from the altar. The angel hurls the censer to the earth, which causes a storm and an earthquake. These signs predict a time of turmoil and stress on the earth. And they introduce the sequence of seven angels with the seven trumpets. The use of seven suggests the gospel age, the age of salvation. The trumpets are a fanfare announcing the seven dramatic eras about to begin.

The first trumpet sounds, and there follows a downpour of fire, hail, and blood. A third of the earth, the trees, and all the green plants is burned up. Green plants suggest living things—perhaps the spiritually alive, or Christians. In the first century of the church's history, Christians suffered severe persecution, first by the Jews and then by the Romans. Jesus had warned that persecution would come and that many Christians would leave the faith (Matthew 24:9, 10). Not all of the trees (strong Christians) would be killed or fall away, but all of the green grass (weak Christians) would be lost.

At the sounding of the second trumpet, what appeared to be a blazing mountain was thrown into the sea. The sea turned to blood, and part of the living things died. Most probably, the symbolism stands for the rapid apostasy (falling away from the faith) of most of the church in the second and third centuries. A mountain, in prophetic language, often means kingdom. Since this mountain is ablaze, it likely stands for the kingdom of light, the church, that spread the message of salvation over the earth in the first generation. The sea is used in Revelation to mean the pagan world. The New Testament church structure was changed into an earthly pyramid of power. It was modeled after the Gentile political organization, not the example of the early church. The simple idea of all believers being priests was changed into a special priesthood limited to an educated clergy.

When the third angel blows his trumpet, a brilliant star falls on the earth's water sources. The rivers and springs all turn bitter, bringing death instead of life. Although students of Revelation have claimed that the fallen star is Satan, this concept does not fit the context. The star here is more likely some historical figure, who appears to hold great hope and promise (a gift from heaven), but who turns out to be the enemy of truth.

> *What Satan failed to accomplish by hardship he began to achieve by prosperity.*

The emperor Constantine fits this idea best. He is known by the world as the first Christian emperor. The church had endured more than a century and a half of persecution by the Roman Empire prior to Constantine's rule. His gestures of good will toward the church were received with great enthusiasm by Christians. When Constantine appeared before the first council of church leaders whom he had convened, the church historian Eusebius said he was "like an angel from heaven."

Constantine repealed all the harsh laws against Christianity. He made Sunday a rest day and began to build church buildings (at church expense). However, all of these advantages came at a very dear price—the loss of personal freedom of conscience. Constantine ruled that church doctrine would be set by councils of bishops. He also said that anybody who taught a different view would be banished from the empire. Religious law now became the law of the state, and the church quickly became a political instrument.

Satan had failed to destroy the church by pagan emperors' cruelty. But now he began to accomplish his aim through Constantine by making the Christian church the official religion of the Roman empire. What Satan failed to accomplish by hardship he began to achieve by prosperity. We have already established this strategy as Satan's second front of attack. Is it possible he's doing the same thing in today's materialistic America?

(For further study concerning Constantine, see Appendix 5, The Two Beasts.)

With the sounding of the fourth angel's trumpet, the sources of light—the living gospel and its preachers—are snuffed out. Truth becomes legislated by the general councils' interpretation of the apostles' tradition. Church history moves into the long twilight of the *apostate church's reign.*

God's Counterattack Begins

The fifth angel sounding his trumpet signaled that another series of events was about to cross the stage of history. First, a star fallen from heaven is given the key to the Abyss (9:1). The Abyss does not represent either hell or Hades. Rather, the Abyss stands for the pagan forces of the huge undiscovered world—the outer wastes of the as yet unknown pagan world. Whether the fallen star is Satan or some historical figure like Constantine is not important in the context. Whoever it represents is God's agent to direct a series of calamities against the seat of the beast, Rome. " *When he opened the Abyss,*

118

Haven't You Heard? There's a WAR Going On! _____

*smoke rose from it like the smoke from a gigantic
furnace. The sun and the sky were darkened by
smoke from the abyss. And out of the smoke locusts
came down upon the earth. . . . The locusts looked
like horses prepared for battle. . . . Their faces resembled human faces. Their hair was like women's
hair"* (9:2, 3, 7, 8).

The agent of God's wrath opens the pit. Out comes
what first appears to be smoke. The smoke turns
into a swarm of locusts with scorpions' stings, and
finally into mounted warriors. God often uses people,
good and bad, to work out his will. He used the
Pharaoh of Egypt and Nebuchadnezzar, king of
Babylon, to accomplish his purposes. He even called
Nebuchadnezzar, "my servant" (Jeremiah 27:6)!

---

*The Commander-in-Chief
himself intervenes in history to
level the field of battle.*

The dramatic sequence of Revelation 9:1-11 portrays God's use of pagan kingdoms to assault the
apostate church. In doing so he preserved the light of
truth just as he did when he used the Assyrian and
Babylonian kings against apostate Israel and Judah.

God has given Christians armor to enable us to
stand against Satan's schemes (Ephesians 4:11) and
he expects us to stand firm and never give in. Sometimes, however, the devil "cuts us off at the pass" by
bringing overwhelming odds against us. In each
circumstance the hills of history flow with "chariots
of fire all around" (2 Kings 6:17) as the Commander-
in-Chief himself intervenes in history to level the
field of battle.

There is no doubt that Satan achieved a crippling victory in the great apostasy. Paul makes this clear in 2 Thessalonians 2:9-12. Satan accomplished it through the great delusion described in Revelation 13 and 17 (chapter 7 of this book). The extent of the deception was "every tribe, people, language and nation" (13:7).

---

*God will use whatever means
necessary, even on a global scale,
to prevent the devil
from achieving a final victory
over us.*

Still, God could not allow such an advantage to fall to the opponents of his people. So, he used his ultimate control over all the earth to unleash a series of debilitating attacks against the beast. This frustrated the consolidation of Satan's kingdom until Christians were again in a position to attack and overcome error.

We should never doubt that God Almighty sits in the command post of history. Clearly God knows every movement of Satan *before* he strikes. This is well-illustrated by his use of barbarian forces to limit the expanding power of Rome. These movements of vast hordes of people began even before the Christian era, but were ready and in place when God needed them. God had already laid plans to outflank Satan. This assurance that God is in charge gives great comfort to his children. But we must never suppose that God is going to take the war out of our hands and fight our battles for us. God will allow us to be tested, but not beyond what we are capable of withstanding (1 Corinthians 10:13).

One truth is abundantly clear: God will use whatever means necessary, even on a global scale, to
prevent the devil from achieving a final victory over
us. Revelation 9 bolsters our faith that "those who
are with us are more than those who are with them"
(2 Kings 6:16). A glimpse at history will help illustrate God's global involvement in our war against
Satan.

The Historical Background

Between A.D. 410 and the last quarter of the sixth
century, Rome suffered a series of barbarian invasions. These attacks first weakened and finally
collapsed the Christian Roman Empire. About 4,000
years before Christ, tribes of large, light-skinned
people began to move south into the Mesopotamian
basin. They are called Caucasians because their
homeland included the Russian Caucasian mountain
region. They left no written history, but archaeolo-
gists have dug up remains of their cities, which were
in Asia Minor during this period. The plain of Shinar
was already settled by Sum-erians and early
Semites (Akkadians). So some of them turned to the
northeast and settled Persia and India and became
known as the Aryans.

Others crossed the Dardanelles until they came to
Scandinavia. Their brief contact with the Semites
may be the source of this statement in Genesis 6:2:
"the sons of God saw that the daughters of men were
beautiful, and they married any of them they chose."
These prehistoric ancestors of the Vikings were
generally much larger than the Semites. The sons of
these mixed marriages became the "heroes of old,
men of renown" (Genesis 6:4).

In Northern Europe, these people became the

Goths. The Goths grew rich and multiplied until they had to find more land on which to live. As they moved southward, these barbarians split into two groups. The Ostrogoths (Eastern Goths) moved onto the Russian steppes. The Visigoths (Western Goths) swung to the southwest and began to put pressure on the Roman Empire. In A.D. 410, Alaric, the chief of the Visigoths, sacked Rome.

Meanwhile, the Ostrogoths had been overrun and forced back into Central Europe by hordes of Huns from the Gobi desert and Mongolia. The Huns attacked Rome in the middle of the fifth century. They demanded tribute, an incredibly high payment as an act of submission to their conquest. Being nomads, though, they did not stay in Rome. They moved on westward until they were finally defeated by the combined armies of Romans and Visigoths in Gaul and by the Poles at Krakow. After their defeat, the Huns disappeared from history, but their bloodline continues in the Turks and Hungarians. Nobody in Europe had known of the Huns before they suddenly appeared. They were agile horsemen who took deadly aim with their bows and arrows. They looked bizarre with long, womanlike hair, strange eyes, and oriental complexions. The Europeans had never seen anything like them and exclaimed, "Where did these things come from—hell?"

Rome was overrun by the Vandals, another barbaric tribe, after the Huns passed on. Then she was defeated by the Ostrogoths and the Lombards (a Germanic tribe). Revelation 9:5 says that they would not destroy the followers of the beast "but only . . . torture them for five months." Perhaps this verse addresses the fact that there were five waves of barbarians that assaulted the Roman Empire in the space of 150 years. The "five" might represent the five invasions and the day-year total of 5 months x

30 days per month equals the 150 years of the barbarian rule.

The Lesson

The message of Revelation 9 is the same to Christians of every age: Don't despair over the *apparent* victories of Satan you witness in the world today. Don't despair over world powers, godless legislation, educational restrictions of religion, or civil laws that conflict with God's Word. These are only dips in the eternal road that lead to final, inevitable victory. God is in control. Christ has already won the war for us. We must do everything possible to remain faithful in our hearts and minds against the attacks of Satan. God always has a counterattack ready to defeat Satan's forces. The crown of life is ultimately ours!

The following information has been included in this chapter for supplemental study. See also Appendix 2, The Four Angels Bound at the Great Euphrates, to find out about the trumpet of the sixth angel.

Barbarian References

In the Revelation text, the "swarms of locusts" (waves of barbarians) are not distinguished from each other. But characteristics of all the barbarian groups can be noted:

1. They were not to harm the grass or any plant or tree—living things (Christians who did not carry the mark of the beast). In fact, the church was not a target of the barbarian conquests, since those peoples had no religious aims.

2. They acted like locust swarms. They ransacked the goods and food supplies but did not kill the people.

3. They "looked like horses prepared for battle." This would particularly describe the Huns, who always fought from horseback.

4. They had stingers in their tails. Both the spears of the Goths and the lances and arrows of the Huns could be described as stingers.

5. They wore "something like crowns of gold" on their heads. This probably refers to the great bronze helmets of the Goths.

124

Haven't You Heard? There's a WAR Going On! _____

6. "Their faces resembled human faces." The bearded faces of both Goths and Huns were surely human, although they were very different from the clean-shaven Romans.

7. "Their hair was like women's hair." Their long hair was remarkable to the Romans and Greeks, whose men had closely cropped or shaven heads.

8. "Their teeth were like lion's teeth." This describes the Huns, who had prominent front teeth. According to some sources, they sometimes filed their teeth to a point.

9. "Breastplates of iron" were worn by both Goths and Huns.

10. "The sound was like the thundering of many horses and chariots rushing into battle." This accurately describes the charge of the Huns' mighty cavalry.

11. "They had as king over them the angel of the Abyss, whose name in Hebrew is Abaddon, and in Greek, Apollyon." Both of these names mean "the Destroyer," which would aptly describe Attila, the leader of the Huns. He boasted of himself, "The grass never grows again where my horse sets its foot."

It is impossible to identify such symbols with historical certainty. Still, the likelihood of Revelation 9:1-11 referring to the period of the barbarian conquests is overwhelming.

Focusing Your Faith

1. List other historical figures, like Attila the Hun, who may be called "agents of God's wrath."

2. Why did the Europeans call the Huns "women from hell"?

3. Who believed "the sword is the key to heaven and hell"? What influence did they have on world religion?

4. What disguises do you see Satan wearing in this chapter? Who is he impersonating?

5. How you feel about God's use of pagan world powers to accomplish his kingdom's purpose? Why?

6. What might be God's purpose for his kingdom in controlling today's world events?

7. Is the true church strong enough today to stand against Satan's infiltration without God's intervention through world events? What can you do to strengthen the church?

Chapter Keys

crown   symbolizes great honor or power unless the context demands another meaning, as in Revelation 9:7.

fire   symbolizes omniscience, sacrifice, or judgment.

golden   denotes something very precious or luxurious.

lamb   is the symbol for Christ—the sacrificial offering for sin.

lamps   stand for truth.

sword   is the symbol of aggressive power, whether good or bad.

throne   represents authority.

white   indicates great age when applied to hair; otherwise it symbolizes purity or sinlessness.

7   symbolizes salvation or the Savior.

Chapter 9

The Ultimate Commander

Images of Christ

~⁊~

Throughout Revelation

Othe devil's
devices in weakening
the resolve of the army
of God is his attempt to
shake our confidence in
the supreme power of
our Commander. One of
the earliest controver-

> ### Key Message:
>
> *The loving Jesus of the gospels is in fact the Commander of the heavenly army and mighty God of the universe.*

sies that wracked the church was the question, "Who
is Christ?" Some argued that he was simply an
exceptionally good man adopted by God into divinity
at his baptism. Many contended that he was only a
created being, inferior in both "substance" and
duration of existence to God himself. These insidious
heresies did much to divide and distract Christian
soldiers from devoting their energies toward the war
of saving the spiritually lost world. They were eventually overcome but at great cost to the unity of the
body.

Then a much more successful attempt was made to undermine Jesus' dignity and his office of mediator between God and man. Mary, the mother of Jesus, was declared to be a perpetual virgin who also had the power of mediating between sinners and God. This demoted Christ to the powerless role of "the infant Jesus."

Revelation 1, 4, and 5 present Jesus as eternal God himself. He is the almighty ruler of all that exists, before all things, and alive forever more. He is at the same time the Lamb of our salvation, and our everlasting High Priest, who holds the scroll of our salvation in his hand. Christians cannot fail in our war against Satan if we follow our Commander-in-chief, "the blessed and only Ruler, the King of kings and Lord of lords, who alone is immortal" (1 Timothy 6:15, 16a) who purchased us with his own blood (Acts 20:28).

> *Although each image is different, each one is an image of the same mighty leader of heaven's armies—God himself.*

John paints several magnificent images of Christ the ultimate Commander in Revelation. These images appear in various forms as the victorious story repeats itself in the cycles of Revelation. Although each image is different, each one is an image of the same mighty leader of heaven's armies—God himself.

These images of Christ the Commander are vastly different from the cooing baby laid in a manger in Bethlehem. They are in great contrast to the gentle,

weeping itinerant preacher who wandered the
Galilean countryside. John presents a breathtaking
encounter with the Risen Lord of all creation—the
mighty I Am, before whose flashing eyes no mere
mortal can stand unassisted.

And yet, John reveals to us in the Holy Spirit, this
awesome, terrible Lord, this fiery-eyed King is also
the one who dried the tears of Mary and Martha,
who raised up the blind Bartimaeus—who allowed
himself to be nailed to a rude cross atop Golgotha.
Why do you suppose he begins his book in such a
fashion?

---

*Satan has viciously attacked
human understanding of both the
full divinity and the full
humanity of Jesus Christ.*

Perhaps it's because we need to see and experience the full reality of our Commander, our Deliverer. Satan's aim is to distract us from Christ's
service, to bedazzle us and detour our walk toward
his presence.

From the Resurrection until now, Satan has
viciously attacked human understanding of both the
full divinity and the full humanity of Jesus Christ. If
he can successfully muddle our minds about either
fullness, then belief in Christ becomes absurd and
salvation is lost to us forever.

Satan's Strategies

The devil has perverted truth to discredit the
fullness of Christ. These lies include:

   • The Gnostic heresy, which had already

started to develop in John's lifetime.
Gnostics argued that the divine spirit
entered into Jesus at his baptism and
left him at the cross. In other words, the
God in Jesus didn't experience human
birth or death. Thus, Christ wasn't fully
human.

- The Arian heresy asserted that Jesus
  was only a created being inferior in
  quality to God himself. The bottom line
  of this teaching was that Christ wasn't
  really God. And if he wasn't God (as he
  claimed to be), his other statements and
  promises would be worthless.

- Attempts in the early Middle Ages tried
  to reduce his person to the "infant
  Jesus" in order to exalt the Virgin Mary
  to the status of mediator.

While none of these plots have completely succeeded, each one has taken its toll on human souls.

---

*God himself dies for us out of his
overwhelming love as our Father.*

Consider the vast theological difference between
these two causes: (1) a human who reluctantly gives
in to divine direction and allows himself to be nailed
to the cross; (2) the Creator of the world who volun-
tarily becomes human in order to die for our sins
according to a plan of love he conceived in eternity.

In the first case, Jesus becomes the hapless victim
of a cruel, manipulative deity—no better or different
than a sheep dog which gives up its life dragging a
mischievous child playing with matches from a

burning house. But in the second case, Jesus becomes a mighty Deliverer—an Almighty God whose infinite love will not permit his creation to suffer. But his infinite justice demands a price for the deliverance—a price which he willingly pays himself.

The Revelation of Christ

John was moved by the Holy Spirit to proclaim the eternal nature of the Word in the opening statement of the Gospel of John. He reinforces that claim in Revelation with a series of images that precisely identify the Lamb—Jesus upon the cross—as the God of eternity, who is the source of all being. In other words, God himself dies for us out of his overwhelming love as our Father.

The Trinity

The early Christians were troubled over both the question of Jesus' identity and the doctrine of the Trinity. Is God one or three? The Jews' central statement of faith was Deuteronomy 6:4: "Hear, O Israel. The Lord our God, the Lord is one." So, the Jews accused the Christians of believing in three gods. The Christians proposed many theories to explain the unexplainable. The most favored explanation became the doctrine of the Trinity, known as the Trinitarian Creed: "God is three persons of the same substance." In actual practice, many Christians rotely repeated the words of the creed but continued to believe this: God was really the Father; Christ was only God in a certain sense because of his relationship to the Father; and the Holy Spirit, that shadowy will-o'-the-wisp, was beyond any rational explanation.

The Book of Revelation and the Gospel of John

contain the "most advanced Christology"—the most precise identification of Christ with God in the New Testament. This chapter discusses some of the reflections of Christ's position and person as described in Revelation.

Image 1: The God of Eternity

Revelation 1

The first image John paints of Christ is a collage of four glimpses of the God of Eternity.

The Alpha and Omega

" 'I am the *Alpha* and the *Omega*,' says the Lord God, 'who is, and who was, and who is to come, the Almighty' " (vs. 8). This statement is all comprehensive. Since alpha and omega are the first and last letters of the Greek alphabet, John is saying that the person addressing him in this passage is the God of Eternity, without beginning or end, the primal cause of all existence, the Creator. The addition of "who is, and who was, and who is to come," identifies the speaker with *Yahweh* of the Jewish *Shema*[1] (Deuteronomy 6:4). Yahweh was the personal name of the God of Israel. Its form was changed to "Jehovah" in the King James Version. Its correct pronunciation is not known because the Jews did not pronounce it, saying "Lord" instead, for fear of

---

[1]The *Shema* (literally, "hear"; pronounced shah-**mah**) is the Jewish confession of faith and a part of every formal service. Early Christians, while not denying the Shema, adopted the practice of saying "Jesus Christ is Lord" (Philippians 2:11). The Muslims repeat one Shema and add, "and Muhammad is his prophet."

blaspheming. *Yahweh* is made up of the Hebrew elements comprising the past, present, and future tenses of the verb "to be." Pronouncing this name was really a way of saying, "The one who has always been, is now, and will forever be."

In Revelation 1:8, however, there is a slight-but-significant change. Instead of "will be," the form has been changed to: "the one who is coming." That expression is messianic. In other words, it refers to the prophesied Messiah and identifies Christ with Yahweh, the God of Eternity. Isaiah 9:6 also states

---

Christ is the eternally complete God who loved us before the beginning of time, throughout earthly history, and loves us for all eternity to come.

---

clearly that the child who was to be born would be called "Mighty God, Everlasting Father." And Paul wrote in 1 Corinthians 10:4 that the spiritual Rock that accompanied the Israelites in the wilderness was Christ. The Rock of the Old Testament was Yahweh, "The Lord is my Rock" (Psalms 18:2; 31:3; 42:9).

Christ, then, is identified as Yahweh. Jesus said of himself, "Anyone who has seen me has seen the Father" (John 14:9), and John wrote of him in the Gospel: "the Word was God" (John 1:1). Where a difference is shown between Jesus and God in Revelation, the difference is not in person, but in his earthly office and his eternal dignity (1:4, 5).

This first image shows Christ as the eternally complete God who loved us before the beginning of

time, throughout earthly history, and loves us for all
eternity to come.

The Ancient of Days

In verses 13 and 14, the Son of Man (Jesus) is
pictured in the garb of the high priest. He has hair
as white as wool and he's standing in the middle of
the seven golden lampstands. This is a reference to
Daniel 7:9 where the Being on the throne—the
Ancient of Days—is also described as having hair as
white as wool. In symbolic language, Revelation is
saying that the person known to history as Jesus
Christ is really the eternal priest and ruler of the
universe. Jesus *is* the Ancient of Days—God himself.

The First and the Last

In verse 17 the Being in the middle of the
lampstands says of himself, "I am the First and the
Last." Revelation 1:12-17 is really a combination of
two Old Testament pictures (see Daniel 10:4-11 and
Isaiah 44:6, 7). In Daniel and Revelation the person
has white hair, feet like bronze, and eyes like fire.
And in both accounts he lays his hand on the
prophet. In Isaiah 44:6 he states (as in Revelation
1:17) "I am the first and I am the last" but adds
"apart from me there is no God." God is the subject
of Daniel 10:4-11 and Isaiah 44:6, 7. But in Revelation 1:17, John identifies Christ as the God of these
Old Testament passages. His point again is that
Jesus Christ is God himself, not some lesser being.

I Am, the Living One

In verse 18 the One speaking to John adds, "I was
dead, and behold I am alive for ever and ever!" This
conclusively shows that the speaker in Revelation is
the post-resurrection Jesus. Isaiah declares him to

be "Israel's King and Redeemer, the Lord Almighty."
And he not only states that he is the Rock, but that
he is the only Rock: "Is there any God besides me?
No, there is no other Rock; I know not one" (44:6-8).
So even in the Old Testament, the Redeemer is
identified as the God who is the Rock. Jesus Christ,
the Rock and Redeemer, is revealed to John as God
himself.

Image 2: The Being on the Throne
Revelation 4–5

John saw a throne in heaven "with someone
sitting on it" (4:2). The throne represents regal
power—a monarch is reigning. This celestial being
has the appearance of jasper[2] and carnelian (probably diamond and ruby).

The jasper and carnelian were the first and last
stones in the breastplate of the high priest—the
"breastplate of prophecy"—suggesting that the
Presence on the throne is the beginning and end of
all prophecy. And we know that Jesus is the sum of
all prophecy.

A rainbow encircled the throne—a symbol of hope
and promise. Since the flood of Noah's time, this
magnificent arch in the heavens has restated the
promise of God to his human creatures. So, the

---

[2]The name "jasper" should not be confused with the
semi-precious stone that bears that name today. It is
simply a rough transliteration of the Greek *yaspes* which
comes from Hebrew *yashpeh*. John states in Revelation
21:11 that the jasper was crystal clear, so the stone
referred to is most probably a diamond. But, the stone's
qualities do not appear to have any relevance here.

rainbow is a particularly fitting symbol of Christ—
God's ultimate Promise. He's the Promise given first
in the garden of Eden and repeated hundreds of
times in the prophets.

This rainbow was not like the usual rainbow,
however, because its spectrum was made up of only
one color—emerald. The significance is not the color
itself but the fact that the emerald was the first
gemstone in the second row of the high priest's
breastplate. It was known to the Jews as the stone of
the tribe of Judah (Exodus 1:2; 28:18). This means
that the King on the throne is of the tribe of Judah.

So from these images we understand that the One
sitting on the throne is the subject of all prophecy,
the Promised One, one who came from the tribe of
Judah. All of these simply confirm that the one
speaking to John is Christ, who reigns forever and
ever.

Image 3: The Lamb That Was Slain
Revelation 5:1-14

John sees a parchment scroll with writing on both
the outside and the inside and sealed with seven
seals. The cross is in the right hand of the One who
sat on the throne. This image probably is taken from
Ezekiel 2:7–3:9. Normally a parchment was written
only on the inside; so, the scroll had to be unrolled to
be read. The unusual thing about the scroll in
Ezekiel and the one in Revelation 5 is that there is
writing on both sides. So, a very limited message
could be read on the outside without unrolling the
scroll. But the complete message could only be
understood after the scroll was unrolled. Since the
scroll is sealed with seven seals (the salvation number), then it contains God's eternal purpose for
saving mankind—the Gospel. The problem is that

nobody on the earth (the living), or under the earth (the dead), or in heaven (angelic beings) are able to break the seals and open the scroll (the age of salvation).

John cries because no one can open the scroll. No one could present us with salvation and John weeps at the realization until he is told by one of the elders (Old Testament prophets and the apostles—the inspired writers), "Do not weep! See, the Lion of the tribe of Judah, the Root of David, has triumphed. He is able to open the scroll and its seven seals." Jacob refers to a lion of Judah (Genesis 49:9), and Isaiah alludes to "a root of Jesse" (Isaiah 11:10). John then sees a Lamb standing in the center of the throne looking as if it had been slain (5:6). The ruler on the throne has volunteered to be sacrificed for man's sins. He stands ready to carry out the order.

The ruler on the throne has volunteered to be sacrificed for man's sins. He stands ready to carry out the order.

The image of the slain Lamb then fades and becomes a Lamb standing before the throne. The Lamb goes to the Being on the throne and takes the scroll. This image shows God/Jesus being separated from his heavenly dignity to take on the form of humanity in order to die for our sins. God is still upon the throne, but God also goes to earth as Jesus of Nazareth: "For in Christ all the fullness of the Deity [Godhead] lives in bodily form" (Colossians 2:9); "God was reconciling the world to himself in Christ" (2 Corinthians 5:19). The Lamb is shown with seven horns and seven eyes. The salvation number is blended with power and knowledge, because Christ has the power and the knowledge to save mankind. He sends the seven spirits—the saving Holy Spirit—to earth to bring the glad tidings of the gospel. As the sacrificial Lamb, God atoned for our sin; in the resurrection, he triumphed over Satan's power to destroy us. Although he was crucified about A.D. 29 in our time, in eternity he is the Lamb slain from the foundation of the world (Revelation 13:8; see also Ephesians 1:4)—slain once for all time. Christ is thus revealed to John as the Lamb whose blood secures eternal deliverance from sin.

Image 4: The Leader of the Heavenly Armies
Revelation 6:1, 2; 19:11-16

Jesus is pictured in Revelation 6:1, 2 as a mighty conqueror riding a white horse and holding a bow in his hand. He rides forth as a warrior king with a crown on his head. In 19:11-16 he is shown riding a white horse with a sword coming out of his mouth. The bow and the sharp sword symbolize the same thing: the power of the word of salvation to conquer sin and Satan and to judge those in rebellion against God. The horse is a symbol of warfare, and its white color is a symbol of purity. All his army also ride white horses. We know that he was given a crown before he rode forth to conquer (6:2).

From Daniel 7:13, 14, we also know that he received his kingdom when he ascended to heaven. Therefore, we know that he conquers during the gospel age and that the heavenly armies are Christians—the church. We are called *heavenly* to distinguish us from earthly or carnal armies.

These following eight points identify the conqueror on the white horse as Jesus:

1. He is faithful and true—19:11 (see also 1:5; 3:7).

2. He has eyes like flames—19:12 (see also 1:14).

3. He is crowned King of kings and Lord of lords—19:12, 16 (see also 6:2; Hebrews 2:9).

4. He has a secret name (the name the Jews considered unspeakable—Yahweh)—19:12. It was the name written on the golden forehead plate of the high priest (Exodus 28:36).

5. He is wearing a robe dipped in blood, a blend of two things involved in the crucifixion—19:13 (see also John 19:24) .

6. He is the Word of God—19:13 (see also John 1:1).

7. The fine linen his followers wear mark them as the church, the bride of Christ. Their robes are made white in the blood of the Lamb (7:7, 8, 14).

8. The sharp sword is the gospel. Christ reveals himself to us, therefore, as Conquering Warrior—19:15 (see also Ephesians 6:17; Hebrews 4:12).

Since he is fully divine and fully human, Christ (God himself) is the only Being qualified to fairly and justly judge mankind.

Image 5: Christ, the Judge of All Mankind
Revelation 19:11; 20:11-15

Since he is fully divine and fully human, Christ (God himself) is the only Being qualified to fairly and justly judge mankind. Having experienced humanity himself, Christ is our defender and perfect representative before the bar of God. And as the

140

Haven't You Heard? There's a WAR Going On! _____

Creator and God of eternity, he alone has the right to render judgment on his creation.

Here are five scriptures that confirm Jesus Christ as the judge of all mankind:

1. Jesus is the one appointed by God as judge of the living and the dead (Acts 10:42).

2. He is the righteous judge (2 Timothy 4:8).

3. The Son of Man will sit on the throne of judgment (Matthew 19:28).

4. On a certain day a "man" appointed by God will judge the world (Acts 17:31).

5. When Christ appears (comes) as king, he will judge the living and the dead (2 Timothy 4:1).

All of us are unquestionably guilty before the throne. But without doubt, we are able to throw ourselves on the mercy of Christ in the eternal court "for his mercy is great" (2 Samuel 24:14b). His mercy is great toward us because God has himself been as fully human as we. He understands us. More remarkable still, he loves us.

The Point of the Images

Through these magnificent images of Christ, we see God himself as the Christ on the cross who saved us. He did not send a substitute to stand human trial and die a criminal's death for us; he came himself. Through these images in John's revelation, he wants us to see him in all his loving, caring, healing, nurturing capacities. He wants us to understand that he himself is the gentle Jesus who loves children, who weeps with his friends, who eats and laughs and walks with us. He is not some far-away, grotesque All-Seeing Eye who merely awaits a reason to "zap" us. He is the sweet Jesus who loved us so much that he took off his heavenly crown and robe of glory. He laid them aside to don the tattered robe of mocking purple and the punishing crown of flesh-tearing thorns. He walked with grim, loving determination the Via Dolorosa to Calvary in our place.

His mercy is great. . . . He under-stands us. More remarkable still, he loves us.

But if he is shown as the Lamb Who Was Slain, he is also shown as the mighty Commander of Heaven's Armies, the Conquering King, the All-Powerful Lord before whom evil cannot stand. To be the first, he must be the second—and vice versa. His mercy is great because of his power, and his power is great because of his mercy (Philippians 2:6-11).

God loved us so much that he came in the form of Jesus Christ and gave himself over to death so that whoever believed in him and his grace could have eternal life. And each image penned by John in Revelation is our own look at God himself, going to the cross for us. Revelation is a personal book written as a letter of love from God.

Focusing Your Faith

1. Suppose you were asked to paint the images of Christ you've seen in Revelation. How would you paint the "God of Eternity—the Alpha and Omega"?

2. When you visualize the image of the Lamb that was slain, how does it make you feel?

3. List the images of Christ from this chapter. Then write one sentence summarizing the personal impact this divine gallery has on you.

4. Imagine that you are standing in front of the Being on the throne. What would you be doing? Remember: You will be doing just that someday.

5. Why should we, as Christians, be happy that Jesus will judge us on the last day?

6. Which of the images of Christ seems the most strange or uncomfortable to you? Why?

7. How can you personally express your gratitude to Christ for his death on your behalf?

Chapter Keys

fire   symbolizes omniscience, sacrifice, or judgment.

Hades   means "not seen." It is the realm or state of the dead and is the equivalent of Hebrew Sheol. It does not mean "hell," although the Hades of Greek mythology was divided into paradise and torment.

sea   symbolizes the pagan world.

throne   represents authority.

white   indicates great age when applied to hair; otherwise it symbolizes purity or sinlessness.

Chapter 10

The Ultimate Victory for the Lord's Army

The Judgment

∞

Revelation 20:11-15

Key Message:

The victory can only be claimed by those who fought in the army of Christ.

Genghis Khan and his Golden Horde will all be there. Hitler and his SS troops, their hands dripping with the blood of the Holocaust, will be held captive by the eyes of the mighty Being on the throne. Adam and Eve, Abraham, Isaac and Jacob will be standing in that throng. Judas Iscariot will be staring helplessly into the blazing eyes of the Judge. And among this incredible assembly will be every faithful soldier of the Cross. Their hearts will surely overflow with joy and gratitude for the immeasurable gift of eternal life.

Nothing can be more awe-inspiring or filled with omens for our eternal future, than thoughts of the great judgment that will take place on the margin of eternity. The earth and the heavens will be no more, but every person who has ever lived will be in that great audience before the Throne.

Every one of us must stand before
a perfect Judge who
will make no mistakes and whose
sentence cannot be changed or
appealed.

"Then I saw a great white throne and him who was seated on it. Earth and sky fled from his presence, and there was no place for them. And I saw the dead, great and small, standing before the throne, and books were opened. Another book was opened, which is the book of life. The dead were judged according to what they had done as recorded in the books. The sea gave up the dead that were in it . . . , and each person was judged according to what he had done. Then death and Hades were thrown into the lake of fire. The lake of fire is the second death. If anyone's name was not found written in the book of life, he was thrown into the lake of fire" (20:11-15).

Daniel also describes that final day of eternal separation of the righteous and the wicked in chilling eloquence:

"As I looked, thrones were set in place, and the Ancient of Days took his seat. His clothing was white as snow; the hair of his head was white like wool. His throne was flaming with fire, and its wheels were all ablaze. A river of fire was flowing, coming out from before him. Thousands upon thousands attended him; ten thousand times ten thousand stood before him. The court was seated, and the books were *opened"* (Daniel 7:9, 10).

Dozens of concepts, from simple to complex, have been proposed to interpret the great judgment scene revealed to John and Daniel. Revelation was obviously inspired to cheer on the Christians of John's time who struggled under the siege of the great war with Satan. Its meaning, then, was surely simple enough for them to grasp. Let's explore this glorious scene and its meaning to Christians of all time.

The Judge

John sees "a great white throne" with an unidentified Presence sitting upon it. Sometimes in the New Testament, God himself is the judge (see Romans 3:6; Hebrews 12:23). Usually, though, Christ is the judge.

John 5:22 says, "The Father judges no one, but has entrusted all judgment to the Son" (see also John 3:37). Acts 10:42 says,". . . [Jesus] is the one whom God appointed as judge of the living and the dead" (see also Romans 14:10). Acts 17:31 reads, "For [God] has set a day when he will judge the world with justice by the man [Jesus] he has appointed."

Actually, it makes no real difference whether the Father does the judging himself or does it through Christ. The vital point is that every one of us must stand before a perfect Judge who will make no mistakes and whose sentence cannot be changed or appealed.

The Time of Judgment

When Jesus Comes Again

Matthew 25:31, 32 says, "When the Son of Man

comes in his glory, and all the angels with him, he will sit on his throne in heavenly glory. All the nations shall be gathered before him, and he will separate the people one from another as a shepherd separates the sheep from the goats."

In the parables Jesus taught that the judgment will take place when he returns (see Matthew 25:1-13; 14-19; Luke 12:35-48).

Following Physical Death

"Just as man is destined to die once, and after that to face judgment, so Christ was sacrificed once to take away the sins of many people" (Hebrews 9:27, 28a).

Following a General Resurrection

"Multitudes who sleep in the dust of the earth will awake: some to everlasting life, others to shame and everlasting contempt" (Daniel 12:2).

Objections to the Doctrine of a General Resurrection

One objection argues that there are two resurrections—the resurrection of the righteous at Christ's coming, and a second resurrection of the wicked after the 1,000-year reign. This view is based on a misunderstanding of Revelation 20:4-6. Being described there is the resurrection from baptism to a new life in Christ (Romans 6:4). The 1,000 years in that passage is the era of the Messiah. It is Christ's reign over his spiritual kingdom, the church. (See chapter 4 of this book for that discussion.)

Another objection to the doctrine of a general resurrection does not take the 1,000 years as a literal time period. It does, though, take the resurrection of Christian martyrs as literal. This view says that those who suffer physical death for the faith will go immediately to heaven, while the rest of the dead will await a general resurrection.

Still others object to a general resurrection because it seems to contradict other passages that appear to say that a soul is taken immediately to eternal destiny at the time of physical death. They cite such passages as Luke 16:22, 23; 23:43; and Philippians 1:22-24 to claim that there is no waiting period between death and the judgment.

_____

Scriptures that seem contradictory to us will be perfectly resolved when we see the whole picture—from our home in eternity.

_____

Part of the difficulty in interpreting the time of judgment stems from our attempt to project a time sequence on a timeless eternity. Since time does not end in eternity, perhaps it is possible that at the point of death (the moment a soul enters a timeless eternity) every soul is *immediately* judged with all men in a general judgment. Suppose a person dies. Their bones may remain in the grave for a thousand years, but for their soul which was *released* from that body, no time whatsoever has passed. Human beings are locked in a temporary state bound by time and space. Nothing in our experience helps us relate to timeless, spaceless eternity. But one thing is certain: the tension between scriptures that seem contradictory to us will be perfectly resolved when we see the whole picture—from our home in eternity.

The Place of Judgment

Not on Earth

"Earth and sky fled from his presence, and there was no place for them" (20:11). "But the day of the Lord will come like a thief. The heavens will disappear with a roar; the elements will be destroyed by fire, and the earth and everything in it will be laid bare [or burned up]" (2 Peter 3:10). Judgment will not take place on earth.

Not in Heaven

All the passages about the judgment imply that the righteous will be invited to enter heaven. So, heaven itself is obviously not the scene of judgment either.

Matthew 25:34 says, "Come, you who are blessed by my Father, take your inheritance, the kingdom prepared for you since the creation of the world."

Verse 23 reads, "Come and share your master's happiness." And verse 10 says, "The virgins who were ready went in with him to the wedding banquet. And the door was shut."

Come and share your master's happiness (Matthew 25:23).

The location of the throne of judgment is not given in Revelation 20. But its implied location is in eternity, between time and the eternal destiny of each person.

Who Is Being Judged?

"The dead, great and small, standing before the throne" are being judged (20:12), including all those who died at sea and all those who were in "death and Hades." Death and Hades were different in Greek thought. Death was the *power* which held the mortal who had departed. Hades was the state or *place* of the dead (Hebrew, *Sheol,* meaning the "pit" or "grave").

The point being made here is that all the dead, whoever they are and wherever they are, will be at the judgment. There will not be one judgment of the righteous and another of the wicked. The resurrection and the judgment to follow are universal. This agrees with Jesus' statement in John 5:28, 29: "A time is coming when all who are in their graves will hear his voice and come out—those who have done good will rise to live, and those who have done evil will rise to be condemned." This does not allow for a "first resurrection" of the righteous, who will reign with Christ for 1,000 years, followed by a resurrection of the wicked. This is, indeed, a once-for-all, general resurrection.

How the Dead Are Judged

Revelation 20:12 says, *". . . and books were opened. . . . The dead were judged according to what they had done as recorded in the books."* It doesn't matter whether these books are literal journals kept by recording angels or simply symbols of the knowledge of an all-wise God. The point is that souls will be judged individually according to how they lived their lives, not by nations or families.

"Another book was opened, which is the book of life" (20:12b). *"If anyone's name was not found*

written in the book of life, he was thrown into the lake of fire" (vs. 15). Notice that no exceptions were made here. People who live their lives in service to others but who do not do it "in the name of Christ"— those who haven't demonstrated obedient faith in him—are not exempt. Those who *claim* to be Christians, but follow a false doctrine not taught by Jesus and the apostles are not exempt. Only those faithful souls who have expressed their faith in Jesus Christ, who have been born again into his family (John 3:3-5; Titus 3:4-7), and who continue to overcome Satan in the daily battle of good versus evil will have their names recorded in the book of life. Only they are exempt from the hideous lake of fire.

The book of life is first mentioned by Moses as "the book you have written" (Exodus 32:32). Unfortunately, it is possible for a human's name to be erased from the book of life (Exodus 32:33; Revelation 3:5). In other words, it is possible for a Christian to fall from grace if he turns his back on God's grace or stops overcoming Satan through the power of Jesus.

Are the Saved Also Judged?

Certain passages seem to teach that *all* men, righteous and wicked, will be judged:

- "But I tell you that men will have to give account on the day of judgment for every careless word they have spoken" (Matthew 12:36).

- "So we will have confidence on the day of judgment" (1 John 4:17).

- The Lord will judge every person (Jude 15a).

- "For we will all stand before God's

judgment seat" (Romans 14:10).

- "For it is time for judgment to begin
  with the family of God" (1 Peter 4:17).

Other passages indicate the righteous will not
undergo judgment:

- "Whoever believes in him is not condemned" [literally, *judged*, in the original language] (John 3:18).

- "Whoever hears my word and believes
  him who sent me has eternal life and
  will not be condemned." [The Greek text
  says, "does not come into judgment"]
  (John 5:24).

Christians will be judged by a "law of liberty."

Still, a general consensus of scripture seems to
teach that all men, righteous and wicked, will appear at the judgment. Christians whose names have
been "blotted out" of the book of life (those who have
fallen from grace), and all who never belonged to
Christ, will be judged according to their evil deeds.
But Christians will be judged by a "law of liberty"
(James 2:12)—freedom from sin through Christ's
blood. In other words, there will be no sins recorded
against them in the books. Their names will be
recorded in the book of life, and Christ will claim
them as his own.

Some believe that even those whose names are
written in the book of life will have their works

judged. This judgment, they say, will not determine whether that soul will be saved, but will determine the degree of their heavenly rewards. This view, however, is difficult to support from Scripture (see Matthew 20).

The Victory Celebration

Imagine, if you can, the judgment scene. The Righteous Judge—Jesus Christ—is sitting in glorious majesty on the throne seat of judgment. Having lived on earth himself, he understands each soul's individual struggles. He desperately wants every one of them to live with him, but his judgment must be holy, righteous, and fair.

To his left is a funeral—a huge throng of people who are screaming for mercy. Their weeping and wailing echo through the halls of eternity. Thick blackness holds them captive. Nothing can save them now—they are eternally sentenced to never-ending misery.

What a victory celebration it is! It's a gathering like no one on earth has ever seen.

But on the other side of the Judge it sounds like a great party. The Judge turns his face toward the sounds of celebration and happiness.

These are his precious ones—the ones who stood with him, against Satan's forces of evil. These are the sweet souls who boldly wore his name, in spite of ridicule and persecution. These are the saints who continually overcame evil and joyfully expressed their gratitude for his grace by doing good things for others. These are the saved who will live with him in heaven forever. Satan has met his eternal doom, and he can never touch them again.

What a victory celebration it is! It's a gathering like no one on earth has ever seen . . . indescribable, incredible, and unending. And the faithful are the guests of honor. Their faces will reflect the majesty and the glory of the King. As each Christian walks toward the Throne wearing a robe made spotless by the blood of the Lamb, Christ himself extends a nail-scarred hand. And he utters a single, blessed, thrilling word—the most precious word a human soul can hear—"Welcome!"

Focusing Your Faith

1. In your mind's eye, when you see yourself standing before the judgment seat of God, what is the expression on your face? Why?

2. What do you hear Jesus, the compassionate Judge, say to you?

3. According to the Bible, when will the judgment be?

4. Where will the judgment take place?

5. Will God's righteous people be judged along with the wicked?

6. Describe the two scenes of judgment—the one to the left of the Judge, and the one to the right.

7. How does it feel to know that you—a Christian who has overcome Satan—are the guest of honor at the eternal celebration hosted by God himself?

Chapter Keys

gold   denotes something very precious or luxurious.

throne   represents authority.

12   is the number of concrete completeness—everyone or everything present and accounted for. Twelve is the symbol for the presence of all God's chosen ones.

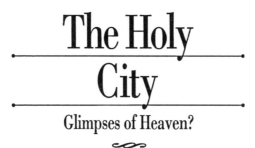

Chapter 11

The Holy City

Glimpses of Heaven?

Revelation 21:1–22:5

A bushman living in the Namibian desert once performed a valuable service for the DeBeers diamond company. As a reward they gave him a trip to the great city of Johannesburg. As he walked along the crowded sidewalks with a guide-interpreter, he was asked what he thought of the towering buildings and glittering arcades. He shrugged and replied, "I don't think anything. They are not real; they are only white man's magic." Soon they passed a site where excavation was in progress for the foundation of a new skyscraper. This giant pit was surrounded by a safety wall. When the little man peeked over the barricade, he almost jumped out of his skin. "Aiee!" he yelled, "That's the biggest hole I ever saw!" He

> **Key Message:**
>
> *The perfect church provides a taste of heaven on earth.*

had finally seen something he could relate to and begin to understand. A skyscraper was, for him, too strange and unbelievable for his frame of reference—so it had to be a mirage. Only when he saw the monstrous hole in the ground—a more familiar concept—could he begin to credit the reality of the concrete-and-steel towers which would soon rise on the construction site.

Men will always have an eager desire to peep through God's keyhole to catch a glimpse of their eternal home.

The kaleidoscope of world cultures all share one constant belief: every tribe on every continent has the conviction that man is more than a mortal creature. They all agree that there is life after physical death. Notions of the nature of that life differ widely according to the values of each culture. Generally, this view of life after death is a glorified vision of the familiarities of earthly society. To the Vikings, for instance, their Valhalla, or heaven, was a place where every day was spent in glorious combat. Wounds received in battle would be healed at sunset so they would be ready to resume fighting the following dawn. To the American Indians, heaven was a happy hunting ground where the supply of deer and buffalo never ran out.

Earthly life, even at its longest, is only a thin slice of eternity. It is certain, then, that men will always have an eager desire to peep through God's keyhole to catch a glimpse of their eternal home. Spiritualists thrive because of the human need to probe the world beyond the grave. They profit greatly by man's need to gain emotional assurance that such a world is really there. People are constantly seeking a window through which to see eternity.

Like the Namibian bushman, people's understanding is limited to concepts rooted in their own experiences. A man may grasp unknown things. Still, the basics of the concept are always fragments of things that already exist. Our limited imaginations, which are confined by earthly time and space, cannot grasp God's timeless, spaceless eternity.

A caterpillar, creeping slowly up a branch and munching green leaves, cannot possibly imagine someday being a butterfly and flying from flower to flower, sipping their delicate nectar. He's so confined by his current inch-by-inch vision, that flying is unthinkable. In the same way, our concept of heaven is defined by our earthly experience.

No Eyewitness Testimony

The Bible is the source of all information, which is acceptable to the Christian, concerning life after death. Men who have returned from the other side—Samuel, Moses, Elijah, and Lazarus—did not give us any eyewitness testimony about the home of the

Our concept of heaven is defined by our earthly experience.

soul. The prophets' visions of heaven (such as Isaiah and Daniel) are so clothed in symbols that they give us no detailed information we can understand. The only section of Scripture that *seems* to give precise information about heaven is Revelation 21 and 22.

For that reason these chapters are the most used and most read chapters in John's book. Whether they truly are a "window upon eternity" we shall explore in the following study.

The Holy City—Is It Heaven?

"I saw the Holy City, the new Jerusalem, coming down out of heaven from God, prepared as a bride beautifully dressed for her husband. And I heard a loud voice from the throne saying, 'Now the dwelling of God is with men, and he will live with them. They will be his people, and God himself will be with them and be their God. He will wipe every tear from their eyes. There will be no more death or mourning or crying or pain, for the old order of things has passed away'" (Revelation 21:2-4).

One wonders whether Lazarus had to go into hiding after his resurrection to escape endless questioning on "what it was like."

The passages in Revelation describing the new Jerusalem are usually thought to describe heaven. That conclusion is based on the following points:

1. The first heaven and the first earth are passed away (21:1);
2. There is no more death, sorrow, or pain (21:4);
3. God and Christ are there (21:22);
4. There is no sun nor moon (21:23);

5. The river of life and tree of life are there (22:1, 2);

6. The saved will reign there forever (22:5).

These are strong arguments. Another reason people find it easy to believe these verses describe heaven is an emotional one. We all have a curiosity about what lies beyond time. It is reassuring to feel that Revelation provides a "knothole" in the wall of silence between us and eternity through which we can take a peek. Paul tells us that "man is not permitted to tell" about heaven (2 Corinthians 12:4). Yet, we still have an itching curiosity about the next life, and naturally so.

One wonders whether Lazarus had to go into hiding after his resurrection to escape endless questioning on "what it was like."

Can Heaven Come Down *from* Heaven?

In spite of our strong desire to have a window on the home of the soul, these problems arise in accepting these verses as a picture of heaven:

1. Understanding Revelation 21 and 22 as a description of heaven does not fit the context of the prophets' writings on which this text is based. That's especially true of Isaiah 30:19; 60:1-3; 65:17-25; Ezekiel 40–48. All of these prophecies are foretelling the reign of the Messiah, when God will set up his tabernacle among men (John 1:14). In other words, in context this is describing the church, not heaven.

2. This city "comes down from heaven." But heaven obviously doesn't come down *from* heaven. This is, rather, describing a heavenly kingdom on earth—a kingdom with a divine origin and character.

3. The foundations of this city are the twelve apostles (21:14). But we know from Ephesians 2:20 that the apostles are the foundation of the church, not of heaven.

4. The gates of this city are still open, and people are coming in (21:24-26). But the gates of heaven will be closed at Christ's second coming (Matthew 25:10).

5. The passing away of the old heaven and earth and the coming of the new illustrates the "new creation" of conversion (2 Corinthians 5:12).

6. The physical sun and moon do not light the church; Christ is the light (Isaiah 2:5; 9:2; 60:1, 3, 19, 20; John 1:9; 8:12).

7. The water of life is salvation through Christ (John 4:10; 7:37, 38; Revelation 22:6). The symbol of the river of life comes from Ezekiel 47:1-12, which describes the life-giving power of the gospel.

In Ezekiel 47:1-12 we have the prophet's version of this same idea. Ezekiel is taken to the entrance of the temple and sees water flowing out from under the threshold.

> *This spring ... clearly refers to the gospel, which spreads from mouth to mouth until it reaches the ends of the earth.*

The Mideast is mostly semi-arid or arid, and water is extremely precious; it symbolizes life and refreshment. Those who forsake the Lord are "like a garden without water" (Isaiah 1:30), but when the anger of the Lord is turned away and he becomes a God of salvation, then "with joy you will draw water from the wells of salvation" (Isaiah 12:3).

"Living water," such as a free-flowing fountain, was a rare thing in the Mideast. It was an historic occasion when Isaac's servants, while digging a well in Gerar, struck a vein of flowing water. It was this kind of flowing spring that Ezekiel sees flowing out of the temple. It's a source of life coming from the throne room of God, but with a notable difference: the flow of most springs gets gradually smaller as the water is absorbed by the dry earth. This spring, though, grows bigger and bigger the farther it flows away from the throne. It is self-multiplying. This clearly refers to the gospel, which spreads from mouth to mouth until it reaches the ends of the earth. There is no contradiction between saying that Jesus is the water of life and the gospel is the water of life, for Jesus is the Gospel. The Man and his Plan cannot be separated. Had there been no Man, there could have been no Plan. Likewise, without the Plan, we would never have known the Man.

In the image of Ezekiel 47, the stream of water grows into a mighty river that eventually empties into the Dead Sea. There, a miracle occurs. Dead creatures in the salty water suddenly spring to life as the fresh water reaches them. Fishermen stand along the banks of the stream and catch the fish in nets. Only the backwaters, where the sweet water cannot reach, remain swamps of death.

This is a beautiful parable of the saving power of the Gospel that can restore the vilest sinner to spiritual life. The fishermen who cast the nets are, of course, those who share the Word, who bring lost souls into the kingdom—a living relationship with God.

8. The greatest problem people have in applying this section of Revelation to the church is reconciling 21:4 with this view. The statement, "He will wipe

every tear from their eyes" is taken from Isaiah 25:8. The implication is not that there will be no tears but that God will wipe them away (compare to Matthew 5:4).

The rest of Revelation 21:4 is taken from Isaiah 65:17-19. In both of these chapters Isaiah is describing the coming messianic kingdom. In other words, he's describing the coming Christ and his kingship in the hearts and lives of his followers. It's the reigning activity of God in our lives as Christians— his kingdom.

The implication is not that there will be no tears but that God will wipe them away. Compare this concept to Matthew 5:4.

---

9. The tree of life is also taken from Ezekiel 47 where it's plural: "fruit trees." Verse 12 says, "Fruit trees of all kinds will grow on both banks of the river. Their leaves will not wither, nor will their fruit fail. Every month they will bear, because the water from the sanctuary flows to them. Their fruit will serve for food and their leaves for healing."

There are several points of similarity between the fruit trees of Ezekiel and the tree of life in Revelation:

- They stand on both banks of the river;
- They are both watered by the water flowing from the throne;
- They both bear fruit every month;
- They both have leaves that are for healing.

However, the application of the two passages seems to be quite different. In Ezekiel the "fruit trees of all kinds" lining the banks of the river seem to fit the "fruits of the Spirit." These are traits in the lives of Christians who have been transformed by the gospel. In Revelation the single "tree of life" seems rather to apply to Jesus Christ himself or, more specifically, to the Cross.[1]

Actually, the only tree given for the healing of the nations and to provide spiritual food is the holy cross of Christ. The healing leaves that come from the tree suggest the shedding of the blood of the Savior. The fruit continuously borne for food suggests the "living bread" (Christ himself, John 6:32-58). This is that bread which came down from heaven, which a man may eat and then live forever.

The Foundations of the Holy City

The twelve foundations of this city each bear the

---

[1]Since these are only symbols, the practical problem of a single tree growing on both sides of the river poses no problem. The word for tree in Revelation 22:2 (as is also true of 2:7) is not the usual word, *dendron*. Instead it is *xulon*. *Dendron* views a tree as a canopy of leafy branches held up by a trunk. *Xulon* sees a tree as a trunk or source of timber. A lumberman might refer to a grove of trees as *xulon* or "a stand of timber." *Xulon* is used for "tree" ten times in the New Testament. Five times it refers directly to the cross of Christ and four times to the tree of life. The tenth time is an obscure allusion in Luke 23:31. There the context shows Jesus on the way to Calvary, and his cross has just been shifted from his own shoulder to that of Simon of Cyrene (Matthew 27:32). For further study see Appendix 4 at the back of this book.

name of one of the apostles (21:14). This illustrates
Paul's statement in Ephesians 2:20 that the church
is built upon the foundation of the apostles who were
prophets. We must not misunderstand what is being
said. The apostles were not personally the foundation of the church. But through them, the gospel
message built the church, based on the "chief cornerstone"—Christ. Ultimately, of course, Christ is the
only foundation of the church (1 Corinthians 3:11).

The image behind the twelve precious stones in
the foundation of the city is the apostles' preaching
as God's instrument to establish the church. These
are the same stones as in the breastplate of the high
priest (Exodus 28:15-21). This garment was called
the "breastplate of prophecy" because it was used
with the sacred onyx stones (the Urim and the
Thummim) for determining the will of God.

The Street of the City

"The great street of the city" (Revelation 22:2) was
made of pure gold as clear as glass (21:21). The river
of life flows down the middle of this street. A street
suggests a going from one place to another and fits
Isaiah's (35:8) description of the Christian life as a
highway called "the Way of Holiness." Gold stands
for something of great value or extremely precious.
As glass is transparent, so the Christ-centered life is
visible to all and has nothing to hide. Not only the
street, but the entire city (the church), is made of
pure gold (21:18). Its walls are of jasper (the original
probably means "diamond"), and its foundation
stones are all precious gemstones.

Like Heaven, the Spiritual Church Is Perfect

There are some major problems in trying to say
that the passages describing the new Jerusalem in

Revelation 21 and 22 refer to heaven itself. Yet, at the same time there's a certain truth to the comparison. Revelation is describing the heavenly character and eternal qualities of Christ's kingdom, the church. It is the ideal church, which is made perfect through her union with Christ. Human minds cannot even imagine a different kind of existence, one where beings are spiritual and immortal. So the closing chapters of Revelation probably give as clear a glimpse of heaven as our minds can grasp.

In spite of the shortcomings we see in the imperfect human beings who make up the physical church, the spiritual church is perfect. It is endowed with the perfect righteousness of Jesus Christ. According to Ephesians 5:27, she is "a radiant church without stain or wrinkle or any other blemish." It's the spiritual garden of Eden where redeemed sinners can once again walk and talk with our God who loves us so much that he died for us. This is why Christians can say with David, "I rejoiced with those who said to me, 'Let us go to the house of the LORD' " (Psalm 122:1).

The church is not a human institution, but a glorious heavenly city, conceived, founded, and established according to the loving grace of God Almighty. It was founded, and must remain founded, upon the inspired teachings of the apostles about Jesus Christ. Inside this holy and wonderful city is heaven on earth. It's a refreshing oasis of peace and joy in the spiritual desert of the world. It's a place of safety—a fortress against her arch enemy, the devil. The church has been sent down from heaven as the overcomer's special place of rest, recreation, and recuperation in the midst of the war.

The Victory

So, the war rages on in the mind and heart of every human being on earth, this great battle of Armageddon. The struggle is for the very soul of man—his eternity in heaven or hell. This magnificent Book of Revelation reveals very clearly that the final outcome of the war has already been decided. Victory belongs to Jesus Christ, the ultimate Commander, the rider on the white horse, the leader of the Lord's army, the one seated on the throne.

What is not determined is this: In which army will we each choose to fight? This decision is entirely in our control. Do we join the 144,000? Do we follow the ultimate Commander who provides peace and security even in the heat of battle? Can we see beyond the trial and trauma of the war to the great prize that is promised in the final victory?

The Lamb of God has already paid the price for each of our names to be written in the book of life. The choice is ours. VICTORY IS IN JESUS.

Focusing Your Faith

1. From this chapter, what is the one constant belief that all people everywhere share? How is that belief interpreted?

2. Would you say that in the eyes of God, we are like caterpillars in some ways? Why?

3. List some of the problems involved with accepting Revelation 21-22 as a description of heaven.

4. Can you see the perfect church in spite of the imperfect people who make it?

5. In this view of God's perfect church, what do you see as its primary thrust? How does that compare to the church as you know it today?

6. Where is the one place on earth we can get a view of what heaven is? Why?

7. If God's church is, perhaps, a bit of "heaven on earth," what songs do you hear us, as its members, singing?

Appendix

Appendix 1

Methods for Interpreting Revelation

There are four more-or-less arbitrary and artificial methods which have been used as the basis for interpreting Revelation in the past.

The Preterist. This method confines the scope of the book to the time and circumstances in which it was written. In other words, its message was only for the late first-century church, and any supposed message for the future is unrealistic.

Historical or Chronological. This method assumes that Revelation is a short summary of church history from the first century to the end of the world. Many of the reformers held this view.

Futurist. The futurist believes that Revelation is primarily concerned with revealing the future, particularly the events immediately preceding the final judgment.

Progressive Parallelism. This view assumes that the message of Revelation was primarily for the church of John's day, but is so broad in scope and its principles so constant that it is relevant for the church of all ages.

Each of these methods of interpretation is partly valid, but you should not be bound by any preset limitations on the scope of your study. Revelation was intended to give hope and comfort to Christians of all ages, but it cannot be used as a crystal ball to unlock the political secrets of the future—nor did John intend for us to try.

Revelation was certainly not intended as a collection of proof texts to establish doctrines not clearly taught elsewhere in the Scriptures.

The Four Angels Bound at the Great River Euphrates
Revelation 9:13-21

"The sixth angel sounded his trumpet, and I heard a voice coming from the horns of the golden altar that is before God. It said to the sixth angel who had the trumpet, 'Release the four angels who are bound at the great river Euphrates.' And the four angels who had been kept ready for this very hour and day and month and year were released to kill a third of mankind. The number of the mounted troops was two hundred million. I heard their number" (vss. 13-16).

In the last half of the sixth century A.D., an uneducated, orphaned, camel boy grew up in Arabia. He was destined to change the world forever, and would be a far greater threat to Europe than either the Goths or the Huns. That camel boy was Muhammad, the founder of the Islamic religion. He claimed to be the prophet of God and declared that his followers would dominate a great portion of the earth. They believed in spreading the new faith by military force, killing or enslaving anyone who would not submit to "the will of Allah." Their rallying cry was, "The sword is the key to heaven and hell!" Muhammad declared that a drop of blood shed in the service of Allah was "worth more than two months spent in fasting and prayer."

Muhammad was, from an early age, very interested in religion. He travelled in the caravans of his uncle's trading business. At night he would listen to debates around the campfires between Jewish and Christian traders over whether Jesus was the

Messiah. But he couldn't understand their failure to come to any agreement. So he got a fairly broad but very shallow knowledge of the Old Testament and the Gospels. He agreed with the Christians that Jesus was born of a virgin and was the Messiah. He totally disagreed with their worship of Mary, which by this time was widespread in the early Catholic church. And he denied their claims that Jesus was the Son of God. He thought it was blasphemy to say that God had a son by a human female.

Each year, Muhammad was accustomed to spending the sacred month of Ramadan in a cave outside the city of Mecca. It was here that he claimed to have received, while asleep, his first revelation from Allah. These alleged revelations took place over a period of twenty years and make up the Quran (also, Koran, the Muhammadan holy book) divided into _surahs_ or "chapters." _Al-Quran_ means "the reading" and represents the messages Muhammad supposedly received in a trance. His teachings which he did not receive while in a trance are called the _Hadith_ or _Sunnah_.

The beginning of Islam is dated from the _Hijrah_ (flight) of Muhammad from Mecca to Medina in A.D. 622. He fled from his enemies in Mecca to Yathrib. There he was hospitably received, and from there he began his conquest of Arabia. He renamed Yathrib _Al-Medina_, which means "the city _par excellence._" Muhammad himself never led any military campaigns outside of Arabia. But his successors—the four caliphs (Abubakr, Omar, Othman, and Ali)— swept through North Africa and the Middle East. They spurred on their troops with the cry, "Before you lies Paradise; behind you is death and hell!"

"The four angels [better translated 'messengers'] who are bound at the great river Euphrates" seem

best to describe the four caliphs who carried Islam
through North Africa and the Middle East. The
Euphrates River is probably an example of synecdo-
che (one part which represents the whole), since
Baghdad, the principal city located on its banks,
would become the political capital of the world of
Islam. Mecca was and is the spiritual capital.

The Pillars of Islam. Islam has no sacraments
and no priesthood. To the average Muslim it consists
of five basic principles called "the five pillars of
Islam," by which he must live:

1. Proclamation of the unity of God: "Allah
   is one God and Muhammad is his
   prophet."

2. Praying five times a day, facing Mecca.

3. Giving alms.

4. Keeping the fast of Ramadan.

5. Making a pilgrimage to Mecca at least
   once in his life, if at all possible.

A Muslim may not eat pork, drink alcohol, gamble,
or charge interest. He is allowed to practice polyg-
amy, which appeals to many pagans, especially in
Africa.

Later Muslim conquests of the eighth and ninth
centuries took them as far as Afghanistan in the
east and into Spain in the west. They crossed the
Strait of Gibraltar in 711 and overran the Visigoths
who had occupied Spain. They were well on the way
toward conquest of Europe from East and West,
until they were stopped at Tours, France, in 732 by
an army of Franks under the leadership of Charles
Martel. They held on in Spain until the fifteenth
century.

The four messengers who had been kept ready in
Revelation 9 were no accidents of unguided history.

They were the agents of God to carry out his justice against perverted Christianity. North Africa had become a stronghold of the Latin church. The Middle East had become the center of the Greek church. Both were corrupt and idolatrous. Admittedly, it is impossible for our mortal minds to understand God's reasons for destroying apostate Christianity, only to replace it with another false religion. But we cannot know what the future holds.

Here are some important points to grasp from Revelation 9:

1. "The four angels were released . . . to kill a third of mankind" (vs. 15). This is probably not to be taken literally, although the slaughter perpetrated by the armies of Islam was horrible. Possibly the reference is to the many converts to a Christless religion— they were spiritually killed (vs. 18).

2. "The number of the mounted troops was two hundred million" (vs. 16). The actual total of Muslim troops during the centuries of their conquests could easily have numbered two hundred million. It seems likely that this is a symbol of a numberless horde.

3. "Their breastplates were fiery red, dark blue, and yellow" (vs. 17). These are reputed to be the colors worn by the Turks. After their conversion to Islam, they became the main fighting force of its armies.

4. "The heads of the horses resembled the heads of lions" (vs. 17). The horses of the Romans and Greeks had cropped manes and tails. The long, flowing manes of the Arabian horses of the Muslims suggest lions' manes.

5. "And out of their mouths came fire, smoke and sulfur. A third of mankind was killed by the three plagues of fire, smoke and sulfur that came out of their mouths" (vss. 17, 18). The horses of the barbarians were described as having stingers only in their

180

Haven't You Heard? There's a WAR Going On! _____

tails [spears, lances, arrows]. The horses of the four messengers caused injury with their tails (vs. 19), but their real power to destroy was in their mouths. In other words, the armies of the Muslims differed in one major way from the barbarian armies: the barbarians destroyed only physically; they had no religious goals. The Muslims pillaged and destroyed physical things and people, too. But their real threat to mankind was what came out of their mouths— false doctrines which separated people from God.

It is clear from the last two verses that the woes announced by the fifth and sixth angels were judgments against a church that had fallen from the faith. "The rest of mankind that were not killed by these plagues still did not repent of the works of their hands; they did not stop worshiping demons, and idols of gold, silver, bronze, stone and wood."

Any false object of worship—a statue of a saint, the Virgin Mary, or even the eternally Infant Jesus—is a false god and a demon. When we attribute magical powers to statues of gold or plaster, we are practicing the equivalent of witchcraft. In fact, idolatry and witchcraft are linked together in Galatians 5:20. Those who worship idols claim that they do not worship the physical statue itself, but the person for whom the image stands. That is a difficult position for them to maintain, since they often ascribe miracles to certain images of the Virgin, or make pilgrimages across the world to pray before a particular statue.

Appendix 3

The Measuring Rod and the Two Witnesses
Revelation 11:1-13

Any project or venture, to be successful, must be pursued according to some plan or set of guidelines. A building contractor cannot erect a structure that will stand if his workmen are simply left to build according to their own whims and fancies.

When God set out to build his spiritual house (the church), he laid the foundation (gave his Son to die), but he depended upon human builders to finish (1 Corinthians 3:10, 11). Each builder is urged to be "careful how he builds" upon it. That implies that there is a definite plan or standard that the builder is supposed to follow with care. God is neither personally giving directions nor supervising us through living apostles today. So the only blueprint we have for building God's temple on earth is his inspired Word. It gives us "everything we need for life and godliness" (2 Peter 1:3). The Bible is the measuring rod by which we can know what God wants his church to be, both as a group and as individuals.

Measuring the Temple of God
Revelation 11:1, 2

"I was given a reed like a measuring rod and was told, 'Go and measure the temple of God and the altar, and count the worshipers there. But exclude the outer court; do not measure it, because it has been given to the Gentiles. They will trample on the holy city for 42 months'" (11:1, 2).

The image here is taken from Ezekiel 40. There

182

Haven't You Heard? There's a WAR Going On!

the prophet's guide to the temple carries a linen cord and a measuring rod. He tells Ezekiel to pay close attention as the guide carefully measures different areas in the temple. Thus, Ezekiel can accurately report what he sees and hears to the people of Israel.

What Is the Measuring Rod?

The account of the measuring occurs in Revelation 11, right after John has been given a little scroll to eat (10:9-11). In Ezekiel the eating of the scroll is told in 3:1-3. In both books, after the prophet eats the scroll he is told to go and preach. The little scroll stands for the new covenant, the gospel, the salvation message.

The scroll John was told to eat was like honey on his tongue but bitter in his stomach. Likewise, the gospel message is a message of joy and hope to those who embrace it, but it's a message of condemnation to those who reject it. It allows no neutral ground. The prophet (or preacher) must preach the results of each of the two options. He cannot pick and choose only the promises; he must also warn of the judgments. The inspired Word is the measuring stick for men's souls in the judgment. So, there is a direct connection between the prophet's receiving a scroll and his receiving a measuring rod. The scroll and the rod are simply different symbols for the same thing—the Word of truth, the only standard by which spiritual things can be measured.

What Is to Be Measured?

John is told by some unidentified person (but probably the angel who had given him the scroll) to rise and measure the temple of God. God's temple is the church (1 Corinthians 3:16; 1 Peter 2:5), but the symbol comes from the Jewish temple in Jerusalem

—forerunner of the church. The temple areas have different names in both Hebrew and Greek.

The entire area, including the outer court called "the court of the Gentiles," comprised the temple precinct called *hekal* in Hebrew and *hieron* in Greek. The sacred enclosure was the area westward from the altar of sacrifice to the holy of holies. Only the priesthood could enter it. Only the high priest could enter the holy of holies, and then but once a year. The enclosure was called *chela* in Hebrew and *naos* in Greek.

When the church is referred to as a temple the word *naos* (shrine) is always used. John is told to measure only the *naos* and is not to measure the outer court of the Gentiles. Among those Gentiles were many "proselytes within the gate." These were nonJews who believed in God and in the Old Testament scriptures. But they refused to become "proselytes of righteousness" by being circumcised.

Ezekiel describes these Gentiles as "Levites who went far from me when Israel went astray." These Levites were allowed to "slaughter the burnt offerings and sacrifices for the people and stand before the people to serve them." God "put them in charge of the duties of the temple and all the work that is to be done in it." But God said they were not allowed "to come near to serve me as priests or come near any of my holy things." He said they "must bear the consequences of their sin" (Ezekiel 44:10-14).

With this combining of Revelation 11:1, 2 and Ezekiel 44:10-14, we may make following application: believers in Christ are divided into two parts. One part is the true church, made up of those souls whose sins have been washed clean by the blood of Christ, who have truly been born again. The other part is made up of those who claim to be Christians.

They have not entered into a saved relationship with Christ, but they still do much good in the world by ministering to people. God uses them to meet the needs of the world, but they do not enter the holy place where the true priesthood ministers.

John is told not to measure the outer court because it is given to the Gentiles. They are not spiritual Israel, but they will dominate it for 42 months. This again is equal to 3 1/2 years which stands for false salvation (3 1/2 is half of 7, which stands for salvation or the saving work of Christ). True Christians, like John, are not to measure them or attempt to usurp God's first right to judge them. The Lord surely "knows those who are his" (2 Timothy 2:19), but no human being is wise enough to make that judgment.

John was told to concern himself only with measuring the *naos* (the holy place, the true shrine). He was told to measure three things: the temple (the church itself), the altar, and the worshipers in it. The New International Version translation reads, "Go and measure the temple of God and the altar, and count the worshipers there." *Count* is not an accurate translation. Temple, altar, and worshipers are all nouns and of the single verb *metreo*—measure. In other words, John was told to measure the church, its worship, and its people by the standards of God's revealed word. In any case, it would be senseless if John were given a measuring rod to count people.

Measuring the Church

First of all, the measuring rod was to be used on the church itself. Therefore, the New Testament itself contains all the standards that are necessary for God's spiritual body to function effectively. The

church is compared to a building in 1 Timothy 3:15;
1 Corinthians 3:10-14; and Ephesians 2:22.

A building is only as sound as its foundation. As
Jesus points out in Matthew 7:24, a wise man builds
his house on rock rather than sand. It doesn't matter
how strong its frame is, a building is no sturdier
than its foundation. The only foundation on which
God's spiritual temple can be built is Jesus Christ
himself (1 Corinthians 3:11). And any religious
system which does not begin with the Son of God is
something different from what Jesus promised to
build (Matthew 16:18). Movements based upon great
figures of history, exclusive cults, or reaction to
controversy are not truly Christ's body. The name on
the church sign or a roll call of all those who claim to
belong in it will not verify that group as Christ's true
church, either.

In the prophet's picture of the temple of God,
Ezekiel is charged to "look carefully, listen closely
and give attention to everything I tell you concerning all the regulations regarding the temple of the
LORD" (Ezekiel 44:5).

Any corporation (whether it is commercial, social,
or spiritual) has specific characteristics. These traits
give that group its individual identity. These traits
are based on the group's charter—the only valid
basis of the body. Paul says in Ephesians 2:20 that
the church is "built on the foundation of the apostles
and prophets."

There is no article (such as "the") with "prophets"
in Ephesians 2:20, indicating that Paul is not making a distinction between apostles and prophets, but
is saying "the apostles who were also prophets."

He is not teaching that it is based upon their
individual dignity and honor or upon their high
position. He is saying that the inspired apostles laid

the foundation of the church by preaching the Cross.
Christ himself is the main foundation—"the chief
cornerstone."

It follows, then, that the true temple of God will be
regulated by the teachings of the inspired Word.
Only upon that basis can it qualify as "the true
tabernacle set up by the Lord, not by man" (Hebrews
8:2).

Measuring the Entrance

Ezekiel was given special instruction to "give
attention to the entrance of the temple" (Ezekiel
44:5). This would be a familiar concept to Jews
because of the warning signs on the "Beautiful Gate"
of Herod's temple. These signs threatened death to
any unqualified person (Gentile) who entered. How
we get into God's temple is of great importance.
According to Ephesians 4:4, 5, membership in the
one body is conditional upon "one Lord, one faith,
one baptism." Any person who has accepted Christ
as his Lord, has responded to the salvation message,
and has been baptized into Jesus' death and resurrection (Romans 6:3, 4) is in Christ's spiritual body,
the church. No human being has the right (or the
ability) to require more or less than that of anyone
seeking salvation.

Measuring Our Practices

Ezekiel's description of the temple of the future is
a prophetic overview of the church. Yet, it's dangerous to apply all its details to the body of Christ. A
prophet's vision is meant to convey general concepts
and ideals, not a specific blueprint to be followed. In
the same way, it's dangerous to make every practice
of the first-century church into a law or pattern for

the church of all time. It depends on whether the
practice itself was essential to the basic principle
being served.

For instance, meeting in an upper room was
convenient for the first-century Mediterranean
culture, but it was not essential to the basic principle of public worship. Some have tried to make
1 Corinthians 16:2 into a command for all time, that
the church must take up a collection every Sunday.
But the practical reason for doing so at Corinth is
clearly stated in the verse: "When I come no collection will have to be made." It was a convenience for
them. Here's the problem with "pattern" theology:
what one interpreter of scripture considers a command, another interpreter considers only a convenience for a particular first-century context. There
will never be total agreement on when an example is
a necessary pattern—a command. We can, however,
agree on this one basic principle:

"Therefore let us stop passing judgment on one
another. Instead, make up your mind not to put any
stumbling block or obstacle in your brother's way"
(Romans 14:13). There is room in the body of Christ
for many viewpoints on matters not clearly stated in
scripture. Even though I may think a brother who
disagrees with me is weak in faith, unity is not
destroyed if I "accept him . . . without passing judgment on disputable matters" (Romans 14:1). The fact
is, he probably thinks I am the one who is weak in
faith. In that case, all I can do is pray for his loving
tolerance of differences on matters of opinion. All
families who love each other tolerate, accept, and
even learn to appreciate the marvelous differences in
each other. We rely on each other's special talents
and insights to make the family function efficiently
and effectively. How much more should this be true

in the family of God, where every Christian's talents and insights are expressions of God himself who lives in us? When we see the beautiful, distinct attributes and viewpoints of other Christians, we are seeing the many facets of our divine Creator, just as the sun's light is reflected in the numerous facets of a magnificent diamond.

The Two Witnesses
Revelation 11:3-14

"And I will give power to my two witnesses, and they will prophesy for 1,260 days, clothed in sack- cloth. These are the two olive trees and the two lampstands that stand before the Lord of the earth" (11:3, 4).

The symbols of the olive trees and lampstands are taken from Zechariah 4:1, 2. The seven-branched golden lampstand or *menorah* used in the tabernacle and in the temple is the basis for this image. The *menorah* gave light to the priests as they carried out their duties in the holy place. It here becomes a symbol of Christ, the light of the world (John 8:12) and his message (the gospel) to the world.

In Zechariah there is only one lightgiver (the Torah or Old Covenant) fed by two olive trees. The light of the lampstand depended on the olive oil as fuel to keep it burning. The sources of the Torah were divided by the Jews into two parts—the law and the prophets. A new dimension has been added in Revelation 11 because there are now two sources of light—the Old and New Testaments. God has given them the power to speak for him. But during the time (1,260 days, 42 months, or 3½ years), the outer court (the religious world in general) is domi- nated by the Gentiles (the unclean priesthood of Ezekiel 44). The message is preached with great

difficulty (in sackcloth and ashes). Anyone who tries
to cut off the sources of truth will be destroyed by
the truth: "That very word which I spoke will condemn him at the last day" (John 12:48).

The gospel had been preached throughout the
world. Then there came a time when the beast (the
fallen church) basically succeeded in cutting off free
access to the Scriptures. The manuscripts still
existed, but men were not allowed to read, translate,
or publish them. In the case of the oldest and best
manuscripts, one of two things happened. They were
either locked away in hiding places, or, in the case of
one of the very best, the Codex Vaticanus, put on
display in a glass case where its "dead body" was on
view, but it could not affect mankind.

God then worked directly to protect the Scriptures
and make them again available. The image of God
taking them up to heaven shows they were put
under divine protection, never again to be denied to
the world. A similar statement is made in Revelation
12:5 about the Christ child being put under divine
protection. In that case, he was protected from
Herod by being taken to Egypt.

After the dark age of ignorance of God's Word (3½
days, half of the seven of salvation), the two witnesses came to life again, much to the chagrin of the
false church. In other words, God's Word began to be
read again. And the Reformation burst upon the
world: "there was a severe earthquake" (11:13). Then
"seven thousand people were killed." That is, seven
(the truly saved) thousand (the true church) were
lost to the false church. Those who remained in the
fallen church gave lip service to God. They only tried
to reform their worst excesses (probably the attempt
by Catholic scholars to reform the church).

The measuring rod and the two witnesses are

symbols for the same thing—the inspired Word. It is the only means by which fallen man can know the saving blood of Christ and be brought to God through Jesus. It is a sad truth that the two witnesses are still dead as far as most of the world is concerned. Hundreds of millions of people living today have never seen a Bible, much less heard the gospel message. They have no divine standard by which to measure their lives and prepare for eternity. It is also a source of deep concern that although the Scriptures are readily available in most of the Western world, most people—even many people who claim to be Christians—do not study the Word carefully.

Special Promises for Those Who Overcome Satan
Revelation 2–3

Periodically, stories surface in the press about the death of some pathetic, friendless soul. Usually, such poor people have been known as eccentric, miserly persons who shunned the company of other humans. How often have we heard the unbelievable testimony of those who have discovered the starved, pitiful remains of such bizarre hermits—stories of drawers full of money, of hidden caches containing thousands of dollars! The poor wretches could have afforded to feast like kings—yet they starved themselves to death, out of some morbid fear of becoming paupers. Their paralyzing fear brought upon them the very fate they dreaded . . . and could have easily avoided.

In some ways, the Christian life is like the dilemma faced by these misguided victims. God has prepared a banquet for each of us, has sent us an engraved invitation to come to his well-laden table. And all too often, we sit at his feasting-board, picking daintily at a few crumbs of joy, when all the time our Host intends for us to be filling ourselves to the bursting with the exuberant, joyful pleasure of his presence. We starve ourselves, and the Lord peers anxiously at us, asking, "Why will you not eat the bounty that I have prepared for you?"

From the second century on, a growing process of extreme self-denial, known as the "ascetic" movement, began to erode the joy of the Christian life as seen in the early church. This process may have come from a gross misapplication of Jesus' statement: "If anyone would come after me, he must deny himself and take up his cross and follow me" (Matthew 16:24). A belief that self-inflicted hardship was the path to holiness led men to deprive themselves of all enjoyable experiences of life. They starved themselves, wore coarse, uncomfortable clothing, and slept on bare stone floors. The concept of cheerless religion was not new. In the previous century, the Pharisees tried to look as miserable as they could to show their piety (Matthew 6:16). But Jesus called them hypocrites.

One of the paradoxes of discipleship is that only by taking on Christ's yoke can we find rest for our souls (Matthew 11:28). We can never be free until we truly become his slaves.

The joy of the Christian life is a major theme in the New Testament. Christians enjoy a priceless fellowship with Christ and each other that is more precious than any earthly treasure. In the letters to the seven churches, Jesus promises rich gifts to his faithful followers. It's important for us to realize that these gifts are not simply future rewards that follow the judgment. They are blessings for right now, shared by Christians who are overcoming sin and Satan in our everyday lives.

Precious Promises for Overcomers

The promises the Lord made to the churches of Asia are generally thought to be heavenly rewards after this life is over. But that does not fit the grammar of the text. Each of the promises is made not "to him who *shall have* [future] overcome," but "to him who *is* [presently] overcoming." This means the reward-giving occurs at the same time that the overcoming is taking place.

Promise to Ephesus:

"To him who overcomes (is presently overcoming), I will give the right to eat from the tree of life, which is in the paradise of God" (Revelation 2:7). The Greek word for "tree" in this verse is *xulon*. This is interesting because it is not the usual word for tree, which is *dendron*. *Xulon* refers to the trunk of a tree and its potential as timber. It is translated "tree" ten times in the New Testament—four times for the tree of life and five times for the cross of Christ. Depending upon how you interpret Luke 23:31, it may be six times for the cross. That strongly suggests a connection, even an identity, between the cross of Christ and the tree of life. Imagine! The Roman instrument of death is transformed into the source of eternal life!

Further, *xulon* is the word used for the tree of life in the garden of Eden (Genesis 3:22, 24, Greek Septuagint). Revelation 2:7 says that the tree of life is in the paradise of God. The word "paradise" suggests a quiet place of rest or a park. The Pharisees called heaven *gan Eden*—the garden of Eden, *pardes*—"paradise" or "Abraham's bosom." The idea of restoration of sweet fellowship between man and God, as in the garden of Eden, was one of the principal expectations for the kingdom of the coming Messiah. The tree of life in Revelation 2:7 is a picture strongly reminiscent of John 6:54-56. We have spiritual life and fellowship with God through the flesh and blood of Jesus, which by faith we partake of. As long as we are overcoming, we have constant access to Christ's sacrifice upon the cross, and the blood shed there continually cleanses us from all sin.

Promise to Smyrna:

"Be faithful, even to the point of death, and I will give you the crown of life" (2:10b). This probably would have reminded John's hearers of the people of Smyrna, who were widely noted for the floral crowns they produced, and wore in honor of the fertility goddess, Cybele. The phrase "of life" identifies the kind of crown—a "life crown." *Eternal life* is the crown which Christians wear. Continuing to wear it is conditional upon our continuing to battle the Evil One (1 John 5:4). The crown can be lost (Revelation 3:11). It becomes an eternal possession only when we are overcomers to the point of death—be it that of a martyr, or a natural death.

Promise to Pergamum:

"To him who overcomes, I will give some of the hidden manna. I will also give him a white stone with a new name written on it, known only to him who receives it" (2:17b). According to Jewish tradition, King Josiah hid the ark of the covenant before his fatal expedition against Pharaoh Necho at Megiddo. When Nebuchadnezzar pillaged the temple—the tradition says, he did not find the ark. The Jews believed the Messiah would find the ark and feed the people from the manna it held. But Jesus identified *himself* as the manna which came down from heaven (John 6:56-58). Our spiritual lives are sustained by "eating the flesh of Jesus" (John 6:54), (not referring to the Lord's supper, of course, but to that which the Lord's Supper commemorates, our spiritual sustenance which comes from Christ,

our crucified Lord).

Promise to Thyatira:

"To him who overcomes and does my will to the end, I will give authority over the nations. . . . I will also give him the morning star" (2:26, 28). Jesus told his disciples after his resurrection: "All authority in heaven and on earth has been given to me. Therefore go and make disciples of all nations . . ." (Matthew 28:18, 19). Jesus was giving authority to his apostles to exercise the power of the gospel to save or condemn all people. The truths of the gospel message are the keys to open the kingdom of heaven to men— the power to free or to bind (Matthew 18:18). The same authority to exercise the power of the gospel was handed down by the apostles to all generations (Titus 2:15; 2 Timothy 2:2)—to us as Christians! When we bring men to Christ through the preaching of the Word, we are extending the rule of God over men's hearts. By so doing, we are exercising authority over the nations. If Christ rules the hearts of men, he then rules the nations through them.

Christ himself says he is the "bright Morning Star" (Revelation 22:16). As the morning star announces the coming of the day, so Christ's coming announced the new day of salvation. One of the prophecies foretelling the coming of Christ says, "A star will come out of Jacob; a scepter will rise out of Israel" (Numbers 24:17).

Promise to Sardis:

"He who overcomes will . . . be dressed in white, I will never blot out his name from the book of life, but will acknowledge his name before my Father and his angels" (3:5). To be dressed in white is to be made clean by the blood of Jesus Christ (Revelation 7:14;

Romans 4:23; Galatians 3:27). It is possible to soil that white robe of righteousness if we give up the struggle against sin and sink back into the wickedness of the world. Only a few Christians in Sardis had kept their righteous clothing unsoiled (Revelation 3:4).

The concept of a heavenly book in which the names of the faithful are written is very old. When God was testing Moses (Exodus 32:9) he said to him, "Now leave me alone . . . that I may destroy them [the Israelites]." Moses pleaded with God that he should forgive them, but added, ". . . but if not, then blot me out of the book you have written." The Lord replied, "Whoever has sinned against me, I will blot out of my book" (Exodus 32:32, 33).

In the great judgment scene of Revelation 20, we find that the book of life is opened to read the names of the saved. This statement is made: "If anyone's name was not found written in the book of life, he was thrown into the lake of fire" (20:15). Whether or not God has a literal book is unimportant. In the mind of God, that greatest and wisest of all computers, every one of his children is registered. "The Lord knows those who are his" (2 Timothy 2:19). However, God will erase any Christian's name who does not continue to overcome sin by following the Lamb.

Jesus promised, "Whoever acknowledges me before men, I will also acknowledge him before my Father in heaven" (Matthew 10:32). Revelation 10:5 repeats the promise. The crucial question is this: When a person's name is read at the judgment, will Jesus acknowledge that person as his? If he does not, then that name is not in the book of life, and that soul will be condemned to everlasting fire.

Acknowledging (confessing) Jesus is much more than saying we believe in his divinity. We confess

him with our entire being—with our lives. Verbally
confessing a belief in him was often a deadly serious
commitment in late New Testament times and for a
century and a half thereafter. Martyrdom was often
the price of admitting to being a Christian. Polycarp,
a disciple of the apostle John and an elder of the
church of Smyrna, was brought before a Roman
magistrate on a charge of being a follower of Christ.
The magistrate was reluctant to condemn an 86-
year-old man and begged him just to say that he
wasn't a Christian. Polycarp exclaimed, "How can I
deny the King who has saved me?" He was immediately tied to a stake and burned alive.

It is rare in today's world that a Christian must
give his physical life for his faith. But in some ways,
we have a much harder course to follow than declar-
ing our belief in Jesus and facing quick execution.
We must consistently acknowledge him with our
attitudes and behavior—living and responding to
human needs in such a God-directed way that men
will say, "There goes a real Christian." Like Paul, we
must "die every day" (1 Corinthians 15:31) by sacri-
ficing our worldly desires and selfish interests to
carry our cross. Then we are truly confessing Christ
in a way that shows the world around us that he is
Lord of our lives. We must die to ourselves—a death
which lasts an entire lifetime.

Promise to Philadelphia:

*"Him who overcomes I will make a pillar in the
temple of my God. Never again will he leave it. I will
write on him the name of my God and the name of
the city of my God, the new Jerusalem, which is
coming down out of heaven from my God; and I will
also write on him my new name"* (3:12).

The temple of God is the body of Christians—the

church (2 Corinthians 6:16). A temple is where a god is worshiped. The temple of the true God is made up collectively of his people because he is worshiped in their hearts. God has promised to make the earnest Christian a pillar in that living temple. This symbol is significant because a pillar both supports the structure and is firmly held in place by that structure. A pillar standing alone may be pushed over by a violent wind, but a pillar that is held in place by a heavy roof is unshakable.

Just so, the person who is vitally involved in the temple—the church—doesn't wander aimlessly in and out. That's why it's so important for every Christian to be actively involved in the ministry of the kingdom. The work of Christ's church is not only important for its own sake; it becomes doubly important in keeping safe the saved. The Christian who is not filling a meaningful role in ministry ends up as an unhappy drifter—a rolling stone rather than a secured, sturdy pillar in God's temple.

"I will write on him the name of my God. . . ." Christians are letters "written not with ink but with the Spirit of the living God, not on tablets of stone but on tablets of human hearts" (2 Corinthians 3:3). We belong to God, and we carry his spiritual brand (Ephesians 1:13; 4:30; 2 Timothy 2:19).

The city of God, the new Jerusalem, is the church (Revelation 21:2, 10). The church should bear a name which reflects her relationship to her Lord. Jesus in his heavenly majesty is the Eternal Word, from everlasting to everlasting. But in his relationship to his people as their Savior, he is Jesus Christ. The word "church" actually comes from the Greek word *kuriake*, which means "of, or pertaining to, the Lord." It translates, however, *ecclesia* which means "assembly" (any assembly, whether social, religious, or political). Early Christians, in order to identify their particular assembly, called it *he kuriake ecclesia*—"the Lord's assembly." In time it was shortened to *he kuriake*—"The Lord's" and so the term "church"grew out of this word.

The "new name" by which God's people were to be called is probably "Christian." The disciples were called "Christians" first at Antioch (Acts 11:26).

It has been suggested that they were given this name in mockery by their pagan opponents. The Greek rendering of the verse, however, removes all doubt. It literally read, "and it occurred that they [Paul and Barnabas] assembled with the church for a whole year, and taught a considerable crowd, and called the disciples Christians first in Antioch." The word for "call" is *chrematizo*, which, as Alfred Marshall points out (in Nestle's *Interlinear Greek-English New Testament*, p. 883) "always (or at least generally) has reference to a divine communication."

Interpreters are not in agreement over whether the "new name" of Isaiah 62:2 is the name Christian, but the use of chrematizo ("divinely called") in Acts 11:26 makes this an interesting possibility.

The Promise to Laodicea:

"To him who overcomes, I will give the right to sit with me on my throne, just as I overcame, and sat down with my Father on his throne" (3:21).

Jesus triumphed over death by his resurrection. Then he sat down with the Father on his throne, having been given all authority in heaven and on earth (Matthew 28:18). He reigns and must continue to reign until he has destroyed his last enemy—death (1 Corinthians 15:26). The weapon he wields is the sharp sword of his word (Revelation 19:15), and he has put that word in jars of clay—human beings,

(2 Corinthians 4:7).

Christians share in the reign of Christ over the nations. We were raised to life from the grave of baptism to share Christ's royal throne (Ephesians 2:4-6).

All of the promises to the seven churches are conditional upon faithful resistance to the devil's temptations. Overcoming is a process, not an attained standard—a climb, not a mountain top. We speak of active and inactive Christians, but an inactive Christian is no Christian at all. We are either overcoming, however feeble and incomplete that struggle may be, or else we have accepted defeat. It matters not at what point in the battle our time span runs out, as long as we are still fighting on the right side when the end arrives. If we have faithfully served in the ranks, the victor's crown was ours from the beginning.

Appendix 5

The Two Beasts
Revelation 13

The First Beast

"And I saw a beast coming out of the sea. He had ten horns and seven heads, with ten crowns on his horns, and on each head a blasphemous name" (Revelation 13:1).

John describes a beast that is a combination of a leopard, a bear, and a lion—three fierce, untamed animals. As in Daniel's parade of four kingdoms (Daniel 7), John sees this three-part beast come up "out of the sea" (the symbol for the nations of the Gentile world). Daniel, on the other hand, sees four separate beasts, which represent four consecutive world kingdoms.[1]

Instead of describing the individual kingdoms as Daniel did, John lumps them all into a single kingdom. And instead of the fourth iron kingdom, John sees seven heads on one beast. This is logical because there was a continuity of world domination beginning with Babylon and ending in the fall of the Roman Empire. During this long year, succession by conquest passed directly from one world empire to the next. It is the fourth world kingdom that is the

---

[1] He actually uses three different sets of symbols (Daniel 2:31-45; 7:2-25; 8:3-25). He identifies the first kingdom as Babylon (Daniel 2:48), the second as Medo-Persia (8:20), and the third as Greece (8:21). The fourth kingdom of iron is never identified by name, but from history we may reasonably infer that it was the Roman Empire.

primary focus of Revelation 13 and 17. And that kingdom is divided into seven phases (or heads).

These heads are described as seven hills and seven kings. The "great city that rules over the kings of the earth" (17:18) sits on the seven hills. This is obviously Rome, which is built on seven hills. Even if one misses the clue of the seven hills, history makes it obvious that the great city which ruled the world in John's time was Rome.

Many scholars have suggested that the seven kings were Roman emperors, but there were, in fact, more than twelve emperors from the time of Julius Caesar until Theodosius, the last ruler of a unified Roman Empire. Rome did, however, live under seven separate governments from the time of the old Latin kings until Christian imperial Rome (from the time of the emperor Constantine[2] forward). That may very well be what is meant in Revelation. John says that five of the seven kings have already passed, a sixth is in existence, and a seventh is still to come. He is writing during the reign of the emperor Domitian, so the sixth kingdom is, perhaps, pagan imperial Rome, and the seventh kingdom could be understood as Christian imperial Rome.

This first beast received the power of the dragon (that is, Satan) and turned men away from God to idolatry. It was typical of ancient pagan religions, particularly in the eastern Mediterranean, that the governmental head of state was worshiped as a god. Statutes of him were usually erected and sacrifices were offered to it.

---

[2] Constantine followed Diocletian as emperor of Rome in the beginning of the fourth century. He made Christianity the Roman state religion and is known in history as the first Christian emperor.

During the time when Revelation was written, for instance, the Roman Caesar was considered a god and had many shrines dedicated to him throughout the empire. This was, of course, blasphemy against the true God. Anyone who refused to make sacrifices to the emperor was executed, and many faithful Christians were killed on that account.

Revelation 13:5 says that the beast has authority for 42 months. Apparently the 42 months mentioned in Revelation 13:5 and 11:2 are the same as the 1,260 days talked about in 11:3 and 12:6. They are also the same as the "time, times and half a time" (3-1/2 years) mentioned in 12:14. The significance of this time is that it's only half of seven (the number of salvation or the gospel age).

The meaning here is that salvation is *promised* but cannot be *attained* through the *false* (apostate) church. The beast does not have the power he claims to have.

One of the heads (governments) of the beast (Rome) appeared to receive a fatal wound (13:3). But the wound was healed, to the utter amazement of the entire world. It is not stated in the text which head was wounded, but obviously it was not one of the heads that had already passed into history. That leaves the sixth head (pagan imperial Rome) or the seventh head (Christian imperial Rome) as possibilities. The end of the pagan empire came at the death of Diocletian. Then, the rise to power of Constantine (the so-called first "Christian" emperor) in A.D. 306 marked a dramatic change. It could be argued that a system had died (received a fatal wound) in one sense but was really reborn as a new Roman Empire. In view of what is written in 13:11-18, however, it's clear that the change is much more fundamental. It's a change from a political empire to a religious empire. The fifth century A.D. is regarded historically as the end of the Roman Empire. John is saying that Rome's "death" is only an illusion; it comes back to life wearing a religious disguise, but it's really the same old empire of Satan. In other words, the devil has gotten religion

The Second Beast

The second beast looks different from the first (13:11). In the first place, his origin is different. The first beast came up out of the sea (13:1)—the pagan world or "many waters" (17:1, 15). The second beast arises from the earth and takes over the authority of the first beast by a subtle disguise rather than by military conquest. This second beast appears as a lamb with two horns. The lamb is the symbol of Christ in Revelation; a horn is the symbol of power. So, this beast looks like Christ and wields two kinds of power (probably political and religious). But the lamb costume is only a disguise, for when the beast speaks, it's the same voice that spoke through the first beast—the voice of Satan.

The second beast is really the seventh head of the dragon, which received the death stroke but came to life again. And it causes the people of earth to worship the first beast—Rome. This imposter lamb uses deception to enslave people, performing great and convincing signs. Paul calls them "counterfeit miracles" that are the work of Satan (2 Thessalonians 2:9-12). Such "miracles" are only convincing to those who reject the truth. The power of this false Christ is so great that he forces his followers to set up a living image in honor of Rome, an image which can both breathe and speak. The beast is a murderous tyrant who compels men (marked on their foreheads) to worship him or at least to serve him

(marked on their right hands), and those who refuse
are killed or prohibited from buying and selling.
They are placed under economic siege.

John then poses a riddle: the number 666, he says,
is the number of the name of the image and the
number of the beast (13:18). The number is not
written in Greek figures, but spelled out: six hundred, sixty and six which are all different letters of
the Greek alphabet; *chai* (written χ), *xi* (written ξ)
and *sigma* (written ς). John says it is man's number—ordinary numerals, in other words.

Many elaborate solutions have been offered to this
riddle: (1) by changing the Greek letters to Hebrew,
it has been made to spell "Nero Caesar"; (2) "The
Latin kingdom" has been suggested, since the numerical sum of the letters in Greek amounts to 666.
It is unlikely that any certain solution can ever be
worked out. Probably the solution is much less
complicated—something that could be understood
(as John suggests) by simply "considering the number." For example: if we write the three letters of the
number, a single symbol appears. The first and last
letters are the first and last letters of *Christos*
(Christ), and the middle letter is the symbol of the
snake χξς. In other words, Christ is on the outside,
but Satan is on the inside. This is another picture of
the beast of Revelation 13:11—a lamb with the voice
of the dragon. More to the point, it's a religious
organization that, in reality, is the same as the old
pagan Roman kingdom. He is the beast who once
was, and now is not, and must come and stay awhile
(17:10). If he is the same as "the lawless one" of
2 Thessalonians 2:3-12, then signs of a great apostasy (a falling away from the true church) were
already beginning to appear in Paul's own time. But
the apostasy would not fully reveal itself until a

later time. When it was fully developed, it would remain until the coming of the Lord Jesus (2 Thessalonians 2:8).

Obviously, the images evoked in Revelation 13 and 17 best fit the Latin church of the Middle Ages. It took, however, several centuries for this church to rise to a position of dominant power. The old Catholic church, from the late second through the sixth centuries, was largely made up of the Greek church. Constantine moved his seat of government from Rome to Constantinople, and religious power was centered in the eastern part of the empire. In fact, when Constantine convened the first of the general councils (Nicea, A.D. 325), of the 300 bishops present, 295 were from the Greek church and only five from the Latin church. From the seventh century onward, the Latin church ascended to the pinnacle of power which resulted in the Holy Roman Empire. Rome was again the seat of absolute power—both religious and political.

Glossary

amillennialism—views the 1,000 years mentioned in Revelation not as a calendar period, but as a symbol for God's reign in the hearts of his people.

Apocalypse—is a Greek word that means "uncovering" or "unveiling." It is translated "revelation" in the first verse of the book of Revelation.

apocalyptic literature—is a type of Jewish-Christian literature in which the theme is developed using symbols and visions. The theme is usually the judgment of God. Parts of the Book of Daniel and several works written during the time between the last book of the Old Testament and the first book of the New Testament contain apocalyptic literature.

Arians—were a heretical group; the followers of Arius (who died in A.D. 336). He denied that Jesus was eternal with the Father. His most quoted statement: "There was a time when the Son was not."

Armageddon—(literally, "Mount Megiddo") refers to a mountain pass near the valley of Esdraelon where many decisive battles were fought in ancient times. So the term would be understood as symbolic of an ultimate struggle between good and evil.

beast—symbolizes a power or institution—political or religious—which is hostile to God and his children (see Daniel 7:3–8:4).

chain—denotes a binding or restricting power.

Constantine—was the first Roman emperor to convert to Christianity. This meant the end of government persecution and a favorable attitude toward Christians by the Roman Empire. But his making religion the law resulted in the reign of the apostate church. He may be represented in Revelation 8:10 as the bright, falling star.

crown—symbolizes great honor or power, unless the context demands another meaning, as in Revelation 9:7.

Domitian—was the Roman emperor from A.D. 81-96. He demanded to be worshiped and he persecuted Jews and Christians who refused. John is thought to have been banished to Patmos during this era.

dragon—represents Satan (see Genesis 3).

earth—is the representation of the world system (or sometimes Judaism when contrasted with sea, but most often as above).

eschatology—means "a study of the last things." This involves everything from Jesus' return to the final destiny of all men.

Eusebius—a Christian who lived in the late third and early fourth century and wrote a *History of the Church,* published in A.D. 325. It is the most important source for learning about many events in the early church.

eyes—are the symbol for knowledge (see 1 Kings 23:43; Zechariah 4:10).

fire—symbolizes omniscience (Revelation 1:14), sacrifice, or judgment.

five months—would be a span of 150 years divided into five periods, because the Hebrews used "days" as symbolic of years (See Genesis 6:3).

Gnostics—were a heretical group in the early church. They believed that the way to God was through a secret knowledge (Greek, *Gnosis*). Gnostics held that material creation was done by an inferior, evil god. So, anything physical was evil. Thus Christ could not have been a real flesh-and-blood man.

Gog—is taken from Ezekiel 38:2, 3. Gog is the leader of the land of Magog. There God's judgment is

described as falling on them. In Jewish writings
between the Testaments, Gog and Magog symbolize
those opposed to the Messiah. Similarly in Revelation, the names represent Satan's forces.

gold/golden—denotes something very precious or
luxurious.

Hades—means "not seen." It is the realm or state
of the dead, and is the equivalent of the Hebrew
Sheol. It does not mean "hell," although the Hades of
Greek mythology was divided into paradise and
torment.

Hellenistic—refers to Greek culture and philo-
sophical outlook. The term comes from *Hellas* which
was the Greek word for the nation we call "Greece."

horns—most often represent powers or kings (see
2 Samuel 22:3; Jeremiah 48:25; Lamentations 2:3,
17; Daniel 8:3-21).

Irenaeus—had been a student of Polycarp, a
personal disciple of the apostle John. Irenaeus
became an influential Christian writer and wrote
Against Heresies to refute the errors of the Gnostics.

key—represents authority. The person with the
key had power over the house or kingdom to open or
close the door.

lamb—is the symbol for Christ—the sacrificial
offering for sin (see also Isaiah 53:7; John 1:29).

lamps—stand for truth (see Psalm 119:105;
Proverbs 6:23).

living creature—represents the Holy Spirit.
"Creature" is a bad translation in the context; "being" is preferable.

Magog—was the land where Gog was leader. See
Gog.

millennium—is a Latin word meaning "1,000
years." There are several views about the 1,000
years mentioned in Revelation 20.

mountain—symbolizes a community of strength—a kingdom (2 Chronicles 20:10; Daniel 2:35; 9:16; Micah 4:1).

Nicea—was a city in Bithynia where a crucial church council was held in A.D. 325 to deal with the Arian controversy. They adopted a creed about the nature and person of Christ which the Arians would not accept. (See also Arians.)

premillennialism—is the view that Christ will return to earth and reign for 1,000 years.

postmillennialism—is the view that Christ will return at the end of a long period in which evil is reduced as the influence of Christianity increases.

morning star—is the herald of the coming day. Likewise, Jesus' coming heralded the coming of the kingdom.

one hour—symbolizes an indefinite time period (see Luke 22:53).

purple—was an extremely expensive dye, and clothing of that color was only worn by royalty or the very rich.

scarlet—was not as expensive as purple but still very costly. The two colors were paired as tokens of royalty.

sea—symbolizes the pagan world (see Daniel 7:3).

serpent—represents Satan (see Genesis 3).

star—served as direction and time constants for the ancients. Therefore, a star symbolized heralds or messengers. They were also considered lesser lights (important, but inferior to the great lights of the sun and moon).

sword—is the symbol of aggressive power, whether good or bad.

throne—represents authority (see Proverbs 20:28; Isaiah 14:13; Jeremiah 3:17).

time, times and half a time—indicates a system

which cannot offer salvation.

waters—is used in various contexts in Revelation for pagan nations, sources of truth; its roaring signifies an authoritative voice.

white—indicates great age when applied to hair; otherwise it symbolizes purity or sinlessness.

Yahweh—is God's personal name in Hebrew, sometimes transliterated as "Jehovah." It is used over 6,000 times in the Old Testament. Most modern translations render it "LORD" in all capitals to distinguish it from "Adonai," the normal word for "Lord."

ziggurat—was a Babylonian temple-tower shaped like a pyramid. They were usually 70 to 160 feet high and often made in seven terraces. The tower of Babel (Genesis 11) is thought to have been a ziggurat.

Zion—originally referred to the hill that is the highest point in Jerusalem. Later it was applied to the city itself. Finally it became a symbol of God's rule over his people through Jesus.

Numbers

3—represents deity.

3 1/2 years—is the same as "time, times and half a time," 42 months, and 1,260 days.

4—is the number of the earth or the material universe.

7—symbolizes salvation or the Savior.

10—represents abstract completeness.

12—is the number of concrete completeness—everyone or everything present and accounted for.

24—is 12 x 2, the number of the patriarchs and of the prophets. In Revelation it was probably used for the Old Testament prophets plus the 12 apostles.

1,000—represents absolute perfection—10 x 10 x 10; completeness infused with divinity.

12,000—is all the saved of one tribe. Twelve (from the analogy of the twelve tribes) is the equivalent of saying "everybody." The 1,000 is the messianic kingdom—the saved. Therefore, all the saved of one tribe is 12,000; the saved of all 12 tribes (i.e., every nation or race) would be 144,000.

144,000—the saved; the church.